DISTANCE L

FEATURED ARTICLES

ON-CAMPUS STUDENTS' PERCEPTION OF DISTANCE LEARNING
Ezra Kiprono Maritim

WEARABLE LEARNING ENVIRONMENTS
Byron Havard, Courtney Hyland, Megan Podsiad, and Nancy B. Hastings

INSIGHTS FROM A REFLECTIVE CONVERSATION AMONG TWO PROFESSORS AND A STUDENT: INSTRUCTIONAL APPROACHES, ACCOUNTABILITY, AND BUILDING COMMUNITY IN ONLINE COURSES
Autumn M. Dodge and Stefanie B. Copp, with Aja Stevens

QUALITY MATTERS: THE IMPLEMENTATION OF A QUALITY ASSURANCE PROGRAM FOR A VIRTUAL CAMPUS AT A STATE COLLEGE IN FLORIDA
Rebekah Wright

GOOGLE CLASSROOM FOR THE ONLINE CLASSROOM: AN ASSESSMENT
Myra Cook Brown

A COMPREHENSIVE MODEL FOR EVALUATING E-LEARNING SYSTEMS SUCCESS
Dimah Al-Fraihat, Mike Joy, and Jane Sinclair

ENDS AND MEANS
Teaching Online Postsecondary Students With a Disability, Chronic Health Condition, or Mental or Emotional Illness: Resources for Instructors
—by Natalie B. Milman

TRY THIS
The Great Pitchman: Selling Distance Learning to the Hesitant Student
—by Errol Craig Sull

ASK ERROL!
—by Errol Craig Sull

AND FINALLY ...
Let's Go Deeply Digital?
—by Michael Simonson

EDITOR
Michael Simonson
simsmich@nova.edu

MANAGING EDITOR
Charles Schlosser
cschloss@nova.edu

ASSISTANT EDITOR
Anymir Orellana
orellana@nova.edu

EDITORIAL ASSISTANTS
Khitam Azaiza
azaiza@nova.edu

Vanaja Nethi
nethi@nova.edu

COLLEGE EDITOR
Eunice Luyegu
eluyegu@nova.edu

ASSOCIATION EDITOR
Reggie Smith
rsmith@usdla.org

PUBLISHER
Information Age Publishing
11600 North Community
  House Road, Ste. 250
Charlotte, NC 28277
(704) 752-9125
(704) 752-9113 Fax
www.infoagepub.com

ADVERTISING
United States Distance
  Learning Association
76 Canal Street, Suite 301
Boston, MA 02114
617-399-1770, x11

EDITORIAL OFFICES
Fischler College of Education
Nova Southeastern
  University
3301 College Ave.
Fort Lauderdale, FL 33314
954-262-8563
FAX 954-262-3724
simsmich@nova.edu

PURPOSE
Distance Learning, an official publication of the United States Distance Learning Association (USDLA), is sponsored by the USDLA, by the Fischler College of Education at Nova Southeastern University, and by Information Age Publishing. Distance Learning is published four times a year for leaders, practitioners, and decision makers in the fields of distance learning, e-learning, telecommunications, and related areas. It is a professional magazine with information for those who provide instruction to all types of learners, of all ages, using telecommunications technologies of all types. Articles are written by practitioners for practitioners with the intent of providing usable information and ideas for readers. Articles are accepted from authors with interesting and important information about the effective practice of distance teaching and learning.

SPONSORS
The United States Distance Learning (USDLA) is the professional organization for those involved in distance teaching and learning. USDLA is committed to being the leading distance learning association in the United

States. USDLA serves the needs of the distance learning community by providing advocacy, information, networking and opportunity. www.usdla.org

NSU's College of Health Care Sciences (CHCS) is the place where compassion and health care meet. At CHCS, the ability to help patients and communities begins with specialized skills developed in our undergraduate, graduate, professional, and postprofessional programs. The demand for health care specialists has never been greater, and CHCS students get a competitive edge in our high-tech clinical simulation labs and surgical suites, which create a real feel for what they will face in the health care profession.

Students in CHCS learn from experienced faculty members who practice what they teach in the health care professions, including anesthesiology, audiology, cardiopulmonary sciences, health sciences, health and human performance, occupational therapy, physician assistant, physical therapy, and speech-language pathology. CHCS programs are conveniently offered on campus and in blended formats.
CHCS—NSU
3200 S. University Drive
Ft. Lauderdale, FL 33328

877-640-0218
http://healthsciences
.nova.edu

INFORMATION AGE PUBLISHING
11600 North Community House Road, Ste. 250
Charlotte, NC 28277
(704) 752-9125
(704) 752-9113 Fax
www.infoagepub.com

SUBSCRIPTIONS
Members of the United States Distance Learning Association receive *Distance Learning* as part of their membership. Others may subscribe to *Distance Learning*.
Individual Subscription: $60
Institutional Subscription: $175
Student Subscription: $40

DISTANCE LEARNING RESOURCE INFORMATION:
Visit http://www.usdla.org/html/resources/dlmag/index.htm

Advertising Rates and Information:
617-399-1770, x11

Subscription Information:
Contact USDLA at
617-399-1770
info@usdla.org

DISTANCE LEARNING
is indexed by the Blended, Online Learning and Distance Education (BOLDE) research bank.

DISTANCE LEARNING MAGAZINE
SPONSORED BY THE
U.S. DISTANCE LEARNING ASSOCIATION,
COLLEGE OF HEALTH CARE SCIENCES,
NOVA SOUTHEASTERN UNIVERSITY
AND INFORMATION AGE PUBLISHING

MANUSCRIPT PREPARATION GUIDELINES

Articles are accepted from authors with interesting and important information about the effective practice of distance teaching and learning. No page costs are charged authors, nor are stipends paid. Two copies of the issue with the author's article will be provided. Reprints will also be available.

1. Manuscripts should be written in Microsoft Word, saved as a .doc file or docx file, and sent on flash drive or CD.

2. *Single* space the entire manuscript. Use 12 point Times New Roman (TNR) font.

3. Laser print two copies of the paper.

4. Margins: 1″ on all sides.

5. Do not use any page numbers or embedded commands. Documents that have embedded commands will be returned.

6. Include a cover sheet with the paper's title and with the names, affiliations and addresses of all authors. High-resolution professional photographs of all authors should be included and should have a file size larger than 500kb.

7. Submit the paper on a flash drive or CD that is clearly marked. The name of the manuscript file should reference the author. In addition, submit two paper copies. Send the digital and paper copies to:

Michael R. Simonson
Editor
Distance Learning journal
Fischler College of Education
Nova Southeastern University

3301 College Avenue
Fort Lauderdale, FL 33314
simsmich@nova.edu

The Manuscript

Word Processor Format
Manuscripts should be written in Microsoft Word.

Length
There is no mandatory length. The average manuscript is between 3,000 and 5,000 words.

Text
Regular text: 12 point TNR, left justified

Paper title: 14 point TNR, centered

Author listing: 12 point TNR, centered

Section headings: 12 point TNR, centered

Section subheading: 12 point TNR, left justified

Do not type section headings or titles in all-caps, only capitalize the first letter in each word. All type should be single-spaced. Allow one line of space before and after each heading. Indent, 0.5″, the first sentence of each paragraph.

Figures and Tables
Figures and tables should fit width 6 ½″ and be incorporated into the document.

Page Numbering
Do not include or refer to any page numbers in your manuscript.

Graphics
We encourage you to use visuals—pictures, graphics, charts—to help explain your article. Graphics images (.jpg) should be included at the end of your paper. Graphic images should be at least 500 kb in size.

Your Advertisement
or Announcement Could Be Here

USDLA
76 Canal Street, Suite 301
Boston, MA 02114
617-399-1770

In Upcoming Issues

Student Profiling, Instructor Use of Mobile Devices, and Device Ownership	Cheng-Chang Pan, Jeffrey A. Graham, and Eunice Luyegu
The Online Master of Science in Applied Economics Program at Georgia Southern University	Richard Blackwood
A DOI Analysis of Distance Education	Loreta Costa and Greta Walsh

On-Campus Students' Perception of Distance Learning

Ezra Kiprono Maritim

Introduction

Through human history, education as a process of knowledge and skills acquisition has neither being confined to one mode of learning or delivery nor to one type of setting. Indeed, its content and delivery has always been dependent on the stage of civilization and the level of technological development. In this context, the evolution of distance learning has been intertwined with human history. This mode of learning became formalized in 1700s, when it was practiced through correspondence education (Harting & Erthal, 2005). Over the years, particularly after the industrial revolution, conventional learning gained more prominence over distance learning across all the societies of the world, its coexistence with distance learning cannot be denied. The coming of printing technology enhanced distance learning through correspondence. Indeed, before the emergence of new technologies in education, the boundaries between the two modes of learning were in relation to time and space, level and control. Today these boundaries have been blurred by technology, leading to convergence of the two modes (Bjarnason, 2004). Today most institutions are embracing open, distance, and e-learning in lieu of the print-based mode. This shift is driven by high cost of print materials and the ubiquitous nature of e-learning.

Globally, the number of students who are enrolling in online learning is increasing. The eight countries leading the way in online education are: United States, India, China, South Korea, Malaysia, United Kingdom, Australia, and South Africa. In the United States, a recent report shows that about 6.3 million students, representing approximately 35% of the university student population, are enrolled in at least one online course (Allen & Seaman, 2017; Betts, 2017; Smith, 2016; Talheimer, 2017). Most of these stu-

Ezra Kiprono Maritim,
Egerton University College of Open Distance and Distance Learning, Mau-Narok Road,
P.O. Box 536-20115, Egerton, Kenya.
E-mail: codl@egerton.ac.ke/
ekmaritim@yahoo.com

dents are undergraduates. The popular distance education programs are in the order of: business and economics; followed by social sciences and applied sciences; third in order are: life sciences, medicine and health, engineering and technology, and humanities and arts. The smallest numbers of distance education programs are recorded in environmental sciences, law, and natural sciences.

ODL DEVELOPMENT IN EDUCATION IN KENYA

In a developing country like Kenya, delivery of education and training is primarily conducted under conventional mode (Kenya Education Network, 2013). Like in other developing countries, where institutions have adopted ODL primarily for teacher training, the print-based mode is the most favorable choice (Perraton, 2010). The use of information and communication technology (ICT) in education and training delivery is both relatively new and low. This situation is dictated by a number of factors that include poor power and Internet connectivity, high cost of information and communication technologies, and poor open and distance learning (ODL) policy at both national and institutional levels (Gunga & Ricketts, 2007; & Republic of Kenya, 2017).

Though open and distance learning is not new in Kenya, the growth of local providers and its acceptance as one of the graduation pathways is relatively new. It entered Kenya's education system during the colonial era, and its e-learning component was incorporated into higher education institutions is late 1990s. For 30 years during postcolonial period, it got stunted. Its reemergence in higher education was by default. This development and transformation of nonelectronic ODL to open and distance e-learning (ODEL) can be put into three overlapping phases.

PHASE 1: COMBINED CORRESPONDENCE AND PRINT-BASED ERA (1960s–1970s)

There were two key ODL players during this era. The first aspect of this phase is characterized by learning that was delivered through correspondence by foreign institutions, mainly from the United Kingdom, led by the University of London, and South Africa, being spearheaded by the University of South Africa. A number of local tertiary institutions facilitated the delivery of ODL programs from these institutions. The target groups were secondary school and university learners. The second segment of this era is characterized by the entry of local ODL players, namely: University of Nairobi established extra mural studies popularly referred to as adult and continuing education.

PHASE 2: COMBINED RADIO AND PRINT MATERIAL ERA (LATE 1960s–1980s)

By late 1960s two successful radio programs supported by print materials were launched by the Ministries of Education and Health and Ministry of Education initiated radio programs for primary and junior secondary schools and in-service training programs for health workers, respectively (Jenkins, 1990a, 1990b). Though these two programs were successful, they were discontinued when the donor funding ended.

PHASE 3: COMBINED PRINT AND E-LEARNING ERA (1990s-TO-DATE)

Though this phase is dominated by a majority of institutions moving to e-learning, there are still institutions that conduct their distance learning by use of print materials. Egerton University established print-based distance learning program with the Ministry of Defence in 1998. The program is offered to this day. Unlike other developing countries, Kenya has never used television to deliver education programs. The e-learning phase has been enhanced by improved electricity and ICT penetration in the country and the legal framework. The two major e-learning catalysts and events that characterized this phase are: the launch of African Virtual University (AVU) and the financial crisis in universities in 1990s.

African Virtual University was launched in 1997 with Kenyatta University and Egerton University being the pioneer partners. This initiative was wholly funded by the World Bank. The inception of AVU marked the first time e-learning entered higher education institutions in Kenya. The AVU programs were delivered via satellite from foreign institutions based in Australia and the United States, namely: Royal Melbourne Institute of Technology, Curtin University, and New Jersey Institute of Technology.

The financial crisis faced by the public universities in early 1990s forced the universities to admit fees paying students to be taught together with government-sponsored students. This income generation strategy was constrained by space limitations and a growing number of full-time employees who needed part-time and evening courses, weekend courses, and face-to-face sessions during vacations in the case of serving primary and secondary school teachers. These emerging market demands forced universities that were established as conventional to turn to open distance and e-learning as a vehicle for increasing the revenue base convert themselves into dual mode institutions, and establish satellite campuses within the country and across the border for purposes of providing semidistance learning. A common phenomenon across all these phases is the inclusion of a face-to-face component.

ODL AND E-LEARNING CHALLENGES AND EMERGING PROSPECTS

The challenges and the prospects of introducing ODL and e-learning as a supplementary and complementary to conventional mode of learning vary from region to region, country to country, and from institution to institution. The primary determinants of ODL and e-learning success in developing countries include acceptability of qualifications by the tutors, learners, and the employers; institutional preparedness in terms of infrastructural investment and human capacity; policy and quality assurance (Kamau, 1999; Siaciwena, 1983; Southern African Development Community, 2004, 2012).

E-READINESS CHALLENGES

While it is fashionable for dual mode institutions of higher learning to be seen to embrace e-learning, one of the major challenges facing Kenya's e-learning providers is their e-readiness. The driving force behind the adaptation of e-learning mode among all the providers in the country is the enhancement of income generation. This at times overshadows the institutions' e-readiness to deliver quality e-learning. Under this situation, many of the providers lack adequate facilities and support services to deliver online programs. For these institutions, the basic entry of the application of e-learning in instructional delivery brought in new infrastructural demands. The dual-mode institutions, which are the bulk of those seeking to be e-learning providers, are at different levels of e-readiness. Kenya Education Network (KENET, 2013) defined e-readiness as "a measure of preparedness of a university or institution to use ICT to enhance the quality of learning, teaching, and research" (p. viii). KENET conducted e-readiness surveys in 2006, 2008, and 2013 in 30 private and public universities in Kenya. Egerton University was one of 30 institutions surveyed.

Oketch, Njihia, and Wausi (2014) pointed out that institutional e-readiness "assessment allows institutions to design systems and put in place appropriate measures that are required for its success. The assessment should include learners' ability to adapt to technological changes, collaborative training and synchronous as well as asynchronous self-paced training" (p. 30). The five categories of e-readiness indicators that KENET (2013) used are: networked access, networked campus, networked learning, networked society, and institutional ICT strategies. From these five categories KENET developed 17 e-readiness indicators. Each indicator was staged on a scale of 1 to 4, where 1 represented unprepared and 4 represented the highest level of preparedness. The 2013 e-readiness survey indicated that:

- Networked PC per 100 students was low. However, this was compensated by large number of students who owned laptop computers.
- Fifty percent of the students who did not have laptops resorted to cyber cafes for computer and Internet access.
- Twenty-five percent of the students assessed computers and the Internet from cyber cafes.
- Seventeen percent of the students accessed computers from their campuses. This indicates that the universities had low computer laboratories.
- Of the 17 e-readiness indicators applied, only two, the ICT in workplace and network environment, scored 3 in a 4-point scale, indicating satisfactory level of e-readiness. These were the only changes in e-readiness between 2008 and 2013. The other 15 indicators scored less than 3 indicating none-readiness.

Interesting issues expressed by students though not in place or available in their universities included:

- Their preference for blended courses.

- Their preference for their instructors to use more learning management systems (LMS) and open content available on YouTube or Khan Academy.

From the survey findings KENET (2013) concluded inter alia that:

- Those universities are still predominantly traditional in their teaching methods and students have little exposure to institutional application of educational technologies.
- Universities still need to invest more in educational technologies and computer laboratories.
- While most universities had ICT policies, implementation of these policies is low.

ODL POLICY AND QUALITY ASSURANCE CHALLENGES

Kenya's poorly articulated policy on ODL only serves the purpose of legitimizing its provision, but is not for enhancing its growth as an alternative mode for the provision of education and training to enhance human resources. ODL remains a peripheral stream in policy recognition. This status exposes ODL provision in the country to vagaries of market forces and institutional exploitation of the learners (Maritim, 2009). While significant resources are generated from ODL streams, these resources are diverted to building facilities such as laboratories for conventional learners. Little funds were plowed back to enhance the learning conditions of distance learners.

Most of the institutions that claim to offer e-learning provide learners with PDF files uploaded to their platforms, compendiums, and sketchy lecture notes. It was only in 2014 when the Commission for University Education came up with guidelines and standards for the provision of distance learning. The presence of a well-articulated national or regional policy gives recognition and creditability to ODL qualifications and creates an environment that promotes positive perception of ODL graduates in the market, harmonization of the provision of ODL in the country and across member states. In Kenya, ODL development has been left to the institution's discretion. While the government education and training policies encourage public universities to utilize ODL to improve access and equity in higher education; it does not provide financial support for infrastructure as in the case of traditional streams, staff salaries or subsidies, running cost, material development, and capacity building (Republic of Kenya, 2005, 2007, 2012).

Sessional Papers No. 1 of 2005 (Republic of Kenya, 2005) and No. 14 of 2012 (Republic of Kenya, 2012) encouraged conventional public universities to expand access and equity in higher education through ODL and e-learning. Sessional Paper No. 14 of 2012 specially states that in addressing expansion of access and equity in higher education the government will implement the following policies: "expand open and distance education (ODL) in universities by leveraging on ICT to take advantage of ICT infrastructure within the country and establish the Open University of Kenya by 2014" (Republic of Kenya, 2012, p. 123). In view of weak policy environment, the establishment of the Open University remains a dream.

The Kenya Vision 2030, the long-term development blueprint for the country, also recognizes the importance of e-learning in scaling up access and equity in higher education. Vision 2030 is very specific and categorical on the need for the utility of ODL and e-learning with respect to enhancing access, equity, and quality of education and training at technical industrial and vocational educational training and university levels. It points out the need to introduce (Republic of Kenya, 2007, p. 85):

- Open and distance learning to enhance access to university education, especially to the financially disadvantaged;
- E-learning and blended learning as an alternative mode of delivery of education in order to improve both access and quality of education.

The policy documents are positive toward the provision of ODL. However, they lack controls on how the institutions should provide ODL. In the absence of a single-mode ODL institution, the provisions of these policy directions are attempts to mainstream ODL in face-to-face institutions. Up to 2012, the institutions that were offering or facilitating foreign institutions to conduct ODL in the country did not have effective quality assurance systems. The 1985 Universities Act had no provision for ODL institutions and programs and hence the quality assurance agency in the country had no legal powers to control the provision of ODL. The role of the facilitating institutions was to receive the study materials from education providers and pass on to the learners, administer examinations, and provide learner support services. The Universities Act of 2012 strengthened quality assurance in both private and public universities. Unfortunately, in most cases, dual mode distance learning providers and the Commission for University Education, the national quality assurance agency, apply in many instances conventional rules and procedures to those who study under nonconventional situations. The pillars and the principles of distance learning include self-pacing and flexibility.

EMERGING E-LEARNING PROSPECTS

The growth in online enrollment in both developed and developing countries has been catalyzed and buttressed inter alia by:

- increase in the number of institutions that are becoming dual mode. In view of advances in ICT, it is now rare to find purely conventional institutions and e-learning has become the "new norm" in institutions of higher learning (Betts, 2017; Bjarnason, 2004; King, 2012; Chen, 2002);
- advances in ICT have brought about convergence of instructional modes in all learning institutions (Bertrand, 2013; Watson, 2008);
- increase in online courses and programs that have been developed primarily for attraction of high enrollment; these courses and programs are accommodating the needs of students in terms of mode, pace, place, and time of study (Friedman, 2018; Smith, 2016);
- increase in the incorporation of online courses into on-campus courses (Carlson et al., 2016);
- increase of virtual universities and "cross-border education" networks (Diallo, Traore, & Fernandes, 2010; Olcott, 2013);
- recognition and accreditation of online courses by international and national quality assurance agencies (Commission for University Education, 2014; Middlehurst & Campbell, 2004);
- diminishing absorption capacity of traditional face-to-face institutions in view of rising student population, in the case of developing countries (Mohamedbhai, 2011);
- Scaling up of learning opportunities through widening access to higher education (Diallo et al., 2010; Garrett & Verbik, 2004);
- decreasing per capita funding to higher education by the national governments called for institutions to resort to the use of ICT for cost effective solutions for increasing institutional resource base by attracting fees paying students (Mohamedbhai, 2011);
- state investments in the Internet infrastructure, especially fiber optic connec-

tivity, thus lowering Internet cost (Andriotis, 2015; Republic of Kenya, 2017);
- increase in competition between telecoms and Internet service providers leading to lower cost and thus resulting in increased adoption of Internet and mobile technologies (Andriotis, 2015); and
- while the growth in online learning looks small in developing countries, except in South Africa, it is still significant given that up to early 2000 many conventional institutions had no ODL streams. Kenya presents a good example of this scenario. In 1963, the official enrollment figures in tertiary institutions only reflect conventional learners. By 2016/2017 academic year, 500,000 students were enrolled in both private and public universities (Republic of Kenya, 2017). Official government statistics classify all university students as if they are all conventional, hence making it difficult to unmask or segregate the few who study online. However, it is estimated that approximately 30,000 were enrolled in online learning, representing 6% of the student population (Kenya Education Network, 2013). The challenge of the number of students studying through distance learning is not unique to developing countries. While reviewing the status of ODL in Europe, Carlson et al. (2016), noted that "student numbers in distance education are difficult to estimate" (p. 28).

Studies from other countries and in-country that have compared the provision of education through e-learning and conventional modes and those of ratings by students of instructions offered on campus and off campus are supportive and persuasive to the introduction of e-learning where resources and other conditions permit. Such studies have found:

- that e-learning tends to outperform classroom instruction (Talheimer, 2017);
- that off-campus students perceive blended learning as creating the largest benefits (Talheimer, 2017). This is because blended learning takes the best of both aspects of real and virtual environments.
- that students prefer blended learning that combines face to face or onsite learning and online, rather than the traditional face-to-face teaching (Kenya Education Network, 2013).
- that older students, women, and full-time employees were more likely to enroll or show preference for distance learning courses over face to face (Harris & Gibson, 2006).
- that students see e-learning as an expected and integral part of the learning process within higher education and where learners get such benefits as ease of access to resources (Concannon, Flynn, & Campbell, 2005).
- that on-campus and off-campus students show no difference in assessment of online instructions and quality (Spooner, Jordan, Algozzine, & Spooner, 1999).

THE PROBLEM

Although the studies from developed countries consistently show e-learning support by both off- and on-campus students, this position might not hold across all learning institutions in developing countries where e-learning is still at infancy. Egerton University, where the study was undertaken, has three campuses: Njoro, Nakuru, and Nairobi. Nakuru and Nairobi were established in early 2000 for income generation through admission of fees paying students. With the emerging concept of "full-time part-time student," the students in these two campuses take their courses both during the day and in the evenings. In view of declining number of fee-paying students

in the last 2 years leading to low fee collection, the university management made a decision in January 2018 to merge these campuses and transfer the students to Njoro campus. The merger process involved consultations with the students as the major stakeholders. The deans and the directors of the faculties affected held a discussion forum with the students. The task of director of the Egerton University College of Open and Distance Learning in these consultations was to disseminate information and highlight to the affected students, the benefits of e-learning mode of study. During the consultations, the students who were affected vehemently rejected being migrated to e-learning mode. One student leader who spoke on behalf of others made two key rejection points by stating that:

1. "We do not want to migrate to e-learning because we want to interact with the lecturers and hence students are saying no to e-learning.
2. In the current trimester system, we complete our 4-year degree programs in 2 and half years."

The statements of student leaders are assumed to reflect the collective opinions of the student population. This reaction to e-learning reflects either lack of knowledge of the functionalities of e-learning platform, the learning management system or a fixation on traditional mode, fear or uncertainty in program completion through this mode. The first statement portraits a picture where students seem not to embrace the obvious benefits of e-learning that includes seamlessness in delivery with respect to learning being placeless, timeless, and borderless; that is, the nature of e-learning being ubiquitous. The software used by Egerton University in e-learning is Moodle. Moodle is an interactive LMS [(also known as a course management system, or virtual learning management environment, or managed learning environment (Holmes & Gardner, 2008; Robb, 2004; Vai & Sosulski, 2011)]. It is an Internet-based medium. The negative implication for those in technologically disadvantaged locations is therefore that the users should be in a place with Internet connectivity. The second ground for the objection to e-learning demonstrates a lack of the concept of learner-centered environment in e-learning course that includes such facets as self-pacing and flexibility. This allows online learners to move quickly through content and, potentially, graduate early. Hence, trimester system is not the only route to early graduation.

The purpose of the present research was to look into how students who have been exposed to the traditional mode of learning in their undergraduate studies think of pursuing their future studies and professional development through ODL. Given the prevailing conditions, where employers no longer release employees for long-term conventional face-to-face training or pursuance of further studies, a large number of the current students undertaking their studies through conventional mode are potential future distance learners and hence their current perception of e-learning helps in the development of e-learning strategies. According to familiarity principle and cognitive dissonance theory (Festinger, 1957), there exists in human beings a consistency in their cognition to develop a preference for practices or objects or perceptions or beliefs that they are familiar with or those that have been exposed to. Under this principle and theory, it was expected in this study that the traditional mode of learning has had a significant exposure effect on the students to the extent of influencing their future choice of mode of study and mindset with a bias toward conventional mode of study.

This study was undertaken in Kenya, where, though the teaching methods at the university level are predominantly conventional face to face, the universities are now investing in e-learning in the hope that this mode will increase both the student numbers and the institution's resource base in future. In such a context, there are a number of technology related challenges at both macro and micro levels. Egerton University, where the study sample was drawn, is the fourth largest public university, with a student population of about 25,000. Though the university has been conducting print-based distance learning since 1998, it launched e-learning programs in the 2014/2015 academic year and approximately 1% of the student population was enrolled in online programs during 2017/2018 academic year.

METHODOLOGY

The overarching question being addressed by this study is: how do students who are following traditional mode of learning and unfamiliar with distance mode perceive ODL as their future mode for further studies and professional development? The study sets out to answer the following sub-questions:

- What aspects of distance learning do on-campus students perceive as attractive?
- What aspects of distance learning do they perceive as repulsive?

SUBJECTS

A sample of 119 students who were enrolled for a diploma in education and bachelor of education (arts-secondary option) at Egerton University volunteered to participate in the study. This included 61 males and 58 females, with age ranging from 18 to 30 years (M age $= 23$, $SD = 2.7$). The majority of participants, 95%, were fourth-year bachelor of education students. Though previous studies have shown gender differences in volunteering, with more females than males tending to volunteer to participate in studies (Musick

& Wilson, 2008), gender differences in participation in this sample did not show a major difference between males and females to warrant concrete evidence for the opposition to such findings.

PROCEDURE

In order to answer the two questions posed in the study, data were collected through a survey method. The survey was carried out between mid-January and late February 2018. This involves administration of the questionnaires to both diploma and Bachelor of Education students. The survey instrument had two parts: open questions and a few closed questions. The closed-questions captured demographic data and questions intended to measure both attractiveness and repulsive factors provided ODL related statements to be responded to by use of Likert-type scale from 1 to 4 (least reason for attractiveness or nonattractiveness; somehow the reason for attractiveness or nonattractiveness; secondary reason for attractiveness or non-attractiveness; primary reason for attractiveness or nonattractiveness).

RESULTS AND DISCUSSION

The analysis of the data was grouped into two major clusters: demographic profile of the subjects and students' future learning preferences.

PROFILE OF THE SUBJECTS

The various e-learning related demographic data gathered from the study subjects in order to remotely gauge their current inclination toward ODL included:

E-READINESS

With the advances in ICT, the communications tools that an ordinary modern university student should have include: smartphone, tablet, laptop, and e-mail address. The ownership of these devices is a good indicator of the students' readiness to take advantage of and adapt to technological changes that are entering the learning environment in higher education institutions. Indeed, at this time and age, the utility of e-learning in learning, teaching, training, and research is taken as a "norm" (Betts, 2017). A good number of the sampled students owned devices that facilitate e-learning, namely:

- smartphone, 20%;
- smartphone and e-mail, 35%; and
- smartphone, laptop and e-mail 27%.

Interestingly, the results show that less than one percent of the students do not own these devices, which is encouraging because this indicates that if e-learning is introduced in a number of education programs and possibly in other programs, students and lecturers will have active engagement. The students' acquired e-readiness is likely to be carried into the future as Oketch et al.(2014) argued that e-readiness is not one-time event and that once the momentum has been achieved the probability of its continuity in future is high.

ODL AWARENESS

Prior to their admission in 2014/2015 academic year, the majority of the students, 88%, were not aware of ODL provision at Egerton University. Interestingly, on the question of the mode of study they could have chosen if they had prior knowledge of ODL existence at Egerton University, equal numbers (44%) would have chosen either mode. In general, this position suggests a positive perception toward ODL.

USE OF LIBRARY E-RESOURCES

The University Library has learning resources in both print and soft forms. For hard copies, the checkout system is in place. The e-resources subscribed by the library are e-books and e-journals, which can be accessed within and outside the campus by both the staff and students. The instrument administered sought to find out the students' awareness of and engagement with the library's e-resources. This awareness was measured by use of a binary choice of 1 = Yes and 2 = No. The results on the level of awareness as indicated as Yes responses to these e-learning resources are as follows: E-books 53% and E-journals 54%. These results are encouraging for a university where it is not mandatory for lecturers to use both conventional and online notes for the teaching their students. This is another indicator of e-readiness. The levels of students' use of electronic devices to access and engage with library e-resources were: smartphones 61%, library computers 59%, laptops 39%, and tablets 8 percent. On the rate of library computer use for access of library resources, it is encouraging that the students are relatively frequent users of library computers.

COUNTERCHECKING QUALITY OF LECTURE NOTES

The import and the impact of ICT in learning is that it enables students to countercheck and compare what they are getting from their lecturers with other sources. Two aspects of this were measured. One was to find out using binary scale of 1=Yes and 2= No whether the students do benchmarking of their lecture notes with other sources. On this aspect, the results indicate that 81% had done the comparison of the lecturer's notes with other sources such as reference books or Internet sources. The other aspect was their self-assessment of the quality of the lectures' notes. On a 4-point Likert scale measure of the comparability in quality of the lecturer's notes with other sources, the responses were as follows:

- lecture notes were of excellent quality, 21%;
- lecture notes were of good quality, 49%;
- lecture notes were of fair quality, 11%; and
- lecture notes were of poor quality, 0%.

This is a positive reflection of quality teaching and satisfaction by the students with what they receive from their lecturers.

From the sample profile, it is clear that though the sample was not distance learners, their e-readiness; their previous lack of ODL awareness of the existence at Egerton University prior to admission to conventional mode; use of their electronic devices to access library e-resources and to countercheck the quality of lecturers' notes suggest the need for Egerton University to buttress these intrinsic motivations by the students by adding the use of ICT into the conventional learning environment. The students appear to be ahead of the university in embracing ICT application in learning.

FUTURE LEARNING PREFERENCES AND REFLECTIONS

Inclination to a particular preferred choice was looked into through identification of enablers of preferred mode; establishment of respondents' readiness to recommend ODL mode to others; their preferred future mode of study; and finally their specific ODL elements that either attract or repulse them in the choice of an ODL mode.

PREFERRED FUTURE STUDY MODE

Upon graduation from a conventional mode, the majority, 88%, preferred continuing their studies through e-learning. Their preferred mode of instruction is that which incorporates a combination of e-learning and traditional face-to-face instruction. This is the same mode recommended by 71% of the respondents for adoption by the university. The stand-alone print-based ODL delivery mode is the least favored option. The blended approach concurs with KENET (2013) survey. The reasons the respondents gave for recommending this blended mode for adoption by Egerton University are summarized below.

1. Pure e-learning is inconvenient to some students, but blended mode is more convenient to all.
2. E-learning component is available anytime (24 hours).
3. Less expensive in terms of fees, accommodation and travel cost.
4. The two methods combined supplement one another:

   - Face-to-face provides the learner with opportunity for clarification of issues/things that may not be clear on e-learning mode.
   - Both address different needs for different learners.
   - Fits everyone's needs.
   - E-learning works for some learning activities and face to face takes care of practical/field experiment and step by step illustration or demonstration or calculation. That is, where a course has a practical component or the content is complex.
   - Face-to-face component/session brings back one from village to campus life-reconnection with campus life.
   - Caters for both the young who prefer traditional face-to-face mode and the working class who favor e-learning mode.
   - Appropriate for slow and fast learners.

5. E-learning makes learning enjoyable and gives up-to-date information.
6. Gives a chance to those involved elsewhere and wish to further their studies.

7. Good for those from some parts of the country without Internet connectivity.
8. E-learning is more efficient for post-graduate studies while the traditional learning is more convenient for undergraduate studies. That is, e-learning is for mature learners who know what they want.
9. Traditional mode alone is time consuming. Traditional mode alone is slow and wasteful.
10. E-learning enhances acquisition of technological skills.
11. Efficiency in time saving with respect to coverage of the content and on resources.
12. E-learning component is placeless and timeless/time-friendly learning.
13. Accountable with respect to tracking learners learning progress.
14. Enhances cultural integration and coexistence.
15. Reduces transitional barriers/borderless.
16. Boosts Egerton University's vision of being a world class university.
17. Global trend. The world is going digital.
18. Egerton is still behind in e-learning.
19. Strike-free. Time is wasted in the institution when lecturers are on strike.

The respondents' recommendations for Egerton University's needs to adopt blended learning reflect several themes. First, these recommendations provide the ground for drawing strategies that an entrant to e-learning environment like Egerton University should take into account. Second, the findings from the present study support previous research that has reported the benefits of e-learning and blended learning (Concannon et al., 2005; Kenya Education Network, 2013; Talheimer, 2017). A number of the reported benefits of e-learning and blended learning mode for learners given in Table 2 are that the learners have the benefits of both real physical contacts with their tutors and the virtual access to learning materials anywhere and anytime.

RECOMMENDATION TO OTHERS

Ones recommendation to a friend or a family member for a course or a program through a specific mode is a reflection and an indicator of his/her positive preference. On a binary choice of 1 = Yes and 2 = No to the question: "Would you recommend a friend or relative to study through any mode of distance learning?," 86% of the respondents responded in affirmative, the recommendations differed on the programs as follows: undergraduate programs 21%, postgraduate programs 66%. This differential preference may be age related, with undergraduate programs attracting younger learners who may also require guidance and mentoring from tutors, while learning by mature learners is intrinsically motivated (Knowles, 1984).

ENABLERS OF PREFERRED MODE

Enablers are those factors that are seen as facilitating preference for e-learning mode of study. These were captured by responses to a question: "What will determine your future choice of your preferred mode of study? The reasons are categorized into four categories according the locus of control, namely:

INSTITUTIONAL FACTORS
- Course duration;
- quality of course content;
- online study/learning mode;
- availability of course/ learning materials/ instructional method in use and accessibility; and
- Internet availability/accessibility to mode of learning/e-learning.

INDIVIDUAL FACTORS
- Undergraduate graduation grade;
- pleasure of studying and working;
- life commitments/self-determination/ family roles;
- learner's interest/mastery/program of interest;
- place of residence/work and distance to the university;
- personnel resources/financial status/ cost; and
- technological tools such as laptops, smartphone.

WORK-RELATED FACTORS
- Availability of time from work and type of occupation/ convenience; and
- kind of business/work/activity involved in.

ODL ATTRACTION AND REPULSIVE FACTORS

In this item, respondents rated on a 4-point Likert scale the reasons they perceived as attracting them to ODL mode and those that they perceived as repulsing them from choosing ODL as their preferred mode of study for further studies and professional development. The rating was based on key elements of ODL that are found in the literature and national and institutional policies. Tables 1 and 2 summarize the levels of attraction and repulsion of ODL elements. DL refers to distance learning.

Interestingly, three factors that stood out to be attracting the respondents to ODL mode are cost of studying, the fact that ODL is technology driven and ODL is a mature-aged friendly mode. Surprisingly, the fact that distance learning is recognized by the Commission for University Education (CUE) and being taught by the same lecturers as those of a conventional stream are not considered as the pulling factors toward choosing ODL mode of study in the future. These findings may be interpreted in view of the courses and the programs they intend to pursue.

The three factors that were identified as repulsive to pursuing studies through ODEL are the heavy dependency of ODEL

Table 1. Level of Attraction to ODL

ODL Elements	1 = Least Reason	2 = Somehow the Reason	3 = Secondary Reason	4 = Primary Reason
DL is recognized by Commission for University Education.	24 (20%	10 (8%)	14 (12%)	22 (19%)
DL is relatively less expensive.	10 (8%)	13 (11%)	19 (16%)	27 (23%)
DL is remotely taught by same university lecturers.	14 (12%)	22 (19%)	15 (13%)	12 (10%)
DL is technology assisted and driven.	9 (8%)	13 (11%)	16 (13%)	32 (27%
DL is mature-aged friendly mode.	13 (11%)	10 (8%)	13 (11%)	26 (22%)

Table 2. Levels of Repulsion to ODL

ODL Elements	1 = Least Reason	2 = Somehow the Reason	3 = Secondary Reason	4 = Primary Reason
DL is a relatively new graduation pathway in Kenya.	27 (23%)	10 (8%)	16 (13%)	19 (16%)
DL is too technology dependent.	14 (12%)	19 (16%)	12 (10%)	25 (21%)
DL is too demanding and rigorous to a learner.	18 (15%)	12 (10%)	19 (16%)	13 (11%)
DL is low in a structured time for study.	18 (15%)	14 (12%)	17 (14%)	11 (9%)
DL is unfamiliar mode for graduates of traditional mode	22 (19%)	12 (10%)	12 (10%)	22 (19%)

on technology, unfamiliarity of ODEL to graduates of conventional stream, and high demands of distance learning on a learner. Technology is reflected as both as an attraction and repulsion factor. This component may be in reference to such factors as poor power and Internet connectivity in some locations in the country where learners may find themselves.

This study was instigated by the position taken by students in one Egerton University campus, Nairobi campus, which was due for closure due to its nonsustainability as a conventional campus. The overall finding was that Njoro campus students did not hold the same views on ODL as the Nairobi campus students as indicated by:

- their willingness to further their studies and professional development through ODL;

- recommendation to others to study through ODL; and
- recommendations to Egerton University to adopt blended learning mode.

The Nairobi campus students' opposition to e-learning may have been a reactionary position to the university's decision to relocate them to Njoro campus rather than their true cognition about ODL mode of learning.

LIMITATIONS

First, the use of volunteers poses limits of this research approach: a weak level of external validity. Second, because the researcher was a class lecturer for the two groups that participated in the study, the results may have been influenced to some extend by the "Hawthorne effect." Third, in addition, this study was conducted in one faculty, the Faculty of Education, and in one university, Egerton University. The university has 10 faculties and Egerton University is a new entrant to the e-learning mode of teaching and learning. Again, this is a situation where external validity is compromised and hence the findings of this research are not generalizable to other faculties and institutions.

Fourth, there is slight difference in situation between Njoro, the study sample group, and Nairobi campus students. In the case of the Nairobi situation, students had the choice of either continuing with what they are familiar with or being forced to the e-learning situation. With students' power, they knew they can change the situation in their favor. They had to publicly deny the benefits of e-learning to achieve their goal of ensuring that the campus is not closed down by the administration. Njoro students were looking into the future and that future might have limited or no options for them.

CONCLUSION

The focus of this study was to find out the preferred future mode of learning of graduates of a conventional mode of learning. The objective of the study was twofold: (a) to identify the aspects of distance learning the on-campus students perceive as attractive and (b) the aspects of distance learning do they perceive as repulsive. While the traditional method of face to face remains dominant at Egerton University (KENET, 2013), as the university becomes a dual-mode institution, it has adopted e-learning in delivering education to a small population of off-campus students. This new approach is yet to be applied to on-campus students as supplementary and complementary to the conventional mode. The principle of familiarity and cognitive dissonance theory would have predicted that those who have been exposed to the conventional mode of learning would prefer

to continue with that approach upon graduation. This study was anchored on these two paradigms. However, this may be an unrealistic position, given the prevailing conditions in the world of work and multiplicity of roles and responsibilities one gets upon graduation. In addition, the diminishing postgraduate opportunities for full-time sponsored study in conventional institutions are becoming a reality, and hence those who seek further studies are forced to seek alternative modes of study. In this respect, the well-established concept of "full-time part-time student" in developed countries is taking root in developing countries.

The results of the study point to the fact that upon graduation from conventional set up, the graduates prefer to continue their further studies and professional development through distance learning, preferably e-learning. It is recommended that Egerton University diversifies a process it has already started, the delivery of instruction through adoption of "blended learning." The study has implications for institutional planning strategies for e-learning, as the indications are that the market forces driving learners to ODL are unlikely to change in the near future. Some of the views expressed by the sampled students for making ODL their preferred study mode have direct implications on e-content development, technology choice, and institutional preparedness. There is one major limitation of this study. The sample was drawn from undergraduate bachelor of education and diploma students, and this may not be a representative of the entire student population in other programs such as law, humanities, science, natural resources, health science, agriculture, commerce, and veterinary medicine.

Finally, much more research will be needed on students' self-reported use of e-books and e-journals in the library. These may be counterchecked with log-ins in the library. The question is: what do students actually search while in the library? This is in view of the general public perception that the current students are not serious users of library resources. This study shows that conventional learners favor ODL for their future studies. Assuming that the fourth limitation stated above brought about this choice, and suppose a condition favorable to conventional mode is created, will ODL still remains their favorable option? In this context, a second study may look at a scenario where the experimenter provides a situation that creates a dilemma in making a choice between ODL and conventional mode of learning. Such an experiment may consider:

Control group being those who undertook their undergraduate studies through ODL and being put in a situation of making a choice between continuing with ODL mode at postgraduate level or changing to conventional mode.

Experimental group being those who undertook their undergraduate studies through conventional mode and being presented with a situation where "a scholarship" is being offered to undertake studies through either ODL or conventional mode.

From cognitive dissonance theory perspective, the question is, "does the offer of scholarship, as a condition or a dilemma that creates a conflict in cognition, make a difference on the choice of the mode of study?"

REFERENCES

Allen, I. E., & Seaman, J. (2017). *Digital learning compass: Distance education enrollment report 2017*. Washington, DC: U.S. Department of Education's National Center for Educational Statistics.

Andriotis, N. (2015). *Importance of e-learning for developing countries*. Retrieved from https://www.efrontlearning.com/blog/2015/03/importance-e-learning-developing-countries.html

Betts, K. (2017). *The growth of online learning: How universities must adjust to the new norm*. Retrieved from https://www.educationdive.com/news/the-growth-of-online-learning-how-universities

Bertrand, L. (2013). Cooperation between distance teaching university and an on-campus university: The creation of dual-mode university. In J. Willems, B. Tynan, & R. Janes (Eds.), *Global challenges and perspective in blended and distance learning* (pp. 115–120). Hershey, PA: Information Science Reference.

Bjarnason, S. (2004). *Mapping borderless higher education: Policy, markets and competition*. London, England: Association of Commonwealth Universities.

Chen Y. J. (2002). The development of cyber learning in dual mode higher education institutions in Taiwan. *The International Review of Research in Open and Distributed Learning, 2*(2).

Concannon, F., Flynn, A., & Campbell, M. (2005). What campus-based students think about the quality and benefits of e-learning. *British Journal of Educational Technology, 36*, 501–512.

Commission for University Education. (2014). *Universities standards and guidelines, 2014*. Nairobi, Kenya: Author.

Diallo, B., Traore, S., & Fernandes, T. (2010). *AVU's experience in increasing access to quality higher education through e-learning in Sub-Saharan Africa*. doi:10.4018/978-1-61520-690-2.ch010

Festinger, L. (1957). *A theory of cognitive dissonance*. Evanston, IL: Row & Peterson.

Garret, R., & Verbik, L. (2004). Transnational higher education: Major markets and emerging trends. In *Observatory on borderless higher education: Mapping borderless higher education policy, markets and competition* (pp. 319–371). London, England: The Association of Commonwealth Universities

Gunga, S. O., & Ricketts, I. W. (2007). Facing the challenges of e-learning initiatives in Africa Universities. *British Journal of Educational Technology, 38*(5), 896–906.

Harris, M. L., & Gibson, S. G. (2006). Distance education vs. face-to-face classes. Individual differences, course preference and enrollment. *Psychological Reports, 98*(3), 756–764.

Harting, K., & Erthal, M. (2005). History of distance learning. *Information Technology, Learning and Performance Journal, 23*(1), 35–44.

Holmes, B., & Gardner, J. (2008). *E-learning: Concepts and practice.* London, England: SAGE.

Jenkins, J. (1990a) Radio language art project, Kenya. In B. N. Koul & J. Jenkins (Eds.), *Distance education: A spectrum of case studies* (pp. 157–162). London, England: Kogan Page.

Jenkins, J. (1990b) Health workers, Kenya. In B. N. Koul & J. Jenkins (Eds.), *Distance education: A spectrum of case studies* (pp. 243–245). London, England: Kogan Page.

Kamau, J. N. (1999, March). *Challenges of course development and implementation in dual mode institutions.* A paper presented as a case study at the Pan Commonwealth Forum on Open Learning, University of Brunei, Darussalam Brunei.

Kenya Education Network. (2013). *The e-readiness survey of Kenyan universities.* Nairobi, Kenya: Author.

King, B. (2012). Distance education and dual mode universities: An Australian perspective. *Open Learning, 27*(1), 9–22.

Knowles, M. S. (1984). *Andragogy in action: Applying modern principles of adult learning.* San Francisco, CA: Jossey-Bass.

Maritim, E. (2009). The distance learning mode of training teachers in Kenya: Challenges, prospects, and suggested policy framework. *The Journal of Open and Distance Learning, 24*(3), 241–254.

Middlehurst, R., & Campbell, C. (2004). Quality assurance and borderless higher education: Findings pathways through the maze. In **Observatory on borderless higher education:** *Mapping borderless higher education policy, markets and competition* (pp. 89–153). London, England: The Association of Commonwealth Universities.

Mohamedbhai, G. (2011). Higher education in Africa: Facing the challenges in the 21st century. *International Higher Education, 63,* 20–21.

Musick, M. A., & Wilson, J. (2008). *Volunteers: A social profile.* Indianapolis, IN: Indiana University Press.

Oketch, H, A., Njihia, J. M., & Wausi, A. N. (2014). E-learning readiness assessment model in Kenya's higher education institutions: A case study of University of Nairobi. *International Journal of Scientific Knowledge, 5*(6), 29–41.

Olcott, D., Jr. (2013). Beyond the boundaries: The future for borderless higher education. In J. Willems, B. Tynan, & R. Janes (Eds.), *Global challenges and perspective in blended and distance learning* (pp. 36–50). Hershey, PA: Information Science Reference.

Perraton, H. (2010). *Teacher education: The role of open and distance learning.* Vancouver, Canada: Commonwealth of Learning.

Republic of Kenya. (2005). *Sessional Paper No. 1 of 2005: Policy framework for education, training and research: Meeting the challenges of education, training and research in Kenya in the 21st Century.* Nairobi, Kenya: Government Printer.

Republic of Kenya. (2007). *Kenya Vision 2030.* Nairobi, Kenya: Government Printer.

Republic of Kenya. (2017). *Economic Survey 2017.* Nairobi, Kenya: Government Printer.

Republic of Kenya. (2012). *Sessional Paper No. 14 of 2012: Reforming education and training sectors in Kenya.* Nairobi, Kenya: Government Printer.

Robb, T. (2004). *Building your own course management system. ETJ Journal, 5*(1).

Siaciwena, R. M. (1983). Problems of managing an external degree programme at the University of Zambia. *Journal of Adult Education. (University of Zambia),* 2(1), 69–77.

Smith, D. F. (2016). *Report: One in four students enrolled in online courses.* Retrieved from https://edtechmagazine.com/higher/article/2016/02/report-one-four-students-enrolled-online-courses

Southern African Development Community. (2004). *Protocol on education and training.* Gaborone, Botswana: Cathay.

Southern African Development Community. (2012). *Regional open and distance learning policy framework.* Gaborone, Botswana: Cathay.

Spooner, F., Jordan, L., Algozzine, B., & Spooner, M. (1999). Student ratings of instruction in distance learning and on campuses classes. *The Journal of Educational Research, 92*(3), 132–140.

Talheimer, W. (2017). *Does e-learning work? What the scientific research says!* Retrieved from http//www.Work-learning.Com/catalog.html

Vai, M., & Sosulski, K. (2011). *Essentials of online course design: A standard-based guide.* New York, NY: Routledge.

Watson, J. (2008). *Blending learning: The convergence of online and face-to-face education.* North

American Council for Online Learning. Retrieved from https://www.inacol.org/resource/promising-practices-in-online-learning-blended-learning-the-convergence-of-online-and-face-to-face-education/

1960–1970: Combined correspondence and print based era
Late 1960s–1980s: Combined radio and print material era
1990s–Today: Combined print and e-learning era

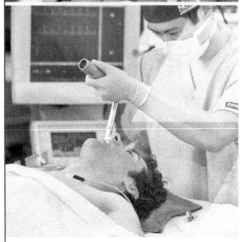

Wearable Learning Environments

Byron Havard, Courtney Hyland, Megan Podsiad, and Nancy B. Hastings

INTRODUCTION AND BACKGROUND

Wearable technologies have progressed over the past decade and have the potential to be used effectively in K–12 classrooms (Lee, Drake, & Williamson, 2015). Wearables have been around since the early 1960s (McCann & Bryson, 2009). Thorp and Shannon created a roulette wheel predictor, a wearable that would predict where the ball would land when playing roulette (McCann & Bryson, 2009). The device did not earn the title of the first wearable until 1966 when Thorp published the work (McCann & Bryson, 2009). Another contributor to wearables was Steve Mann. Mann developed his first wearable system in the early 1980s, and it was composed of a head-mounted camera and a backpack (Mann, 1997; McCann & Bryson, 2009). Over the next 20 years, Mann's (1997) wearable continued to evolve into a less cumbersome device.

In the late 1980s and early 1990s, further progress in the area of wearable technology made smart glasses commercially available (Havard & Podsiad, 2017). After the introduction of the World Wide Web,

Byron Havard,
University of West Florida, Instructional Design and Technology, 11000 University Parkway, Bldg. 85/118, Pensacola, FL 32514.
Telephone: (850) 474-2952.
E-mail: bhavard@uwf.edu

Courtney Hyland,
University of West Florida,
Instructional Design and Technology,
11000 University Parkway, Bldg. 85/114,
Pensacola, FL 32514.
E-mail: ch67@students.uwf.edu

researchers began sharing their wearable computing studies internationally (McCann & Bryson, 2009). The sharing of information enabled technology developers to combine the ideas of multiple wearables to create new technologies. In 1993, Platt and Starner combined smart glasses called the Private Eye and a one-handed keyboard to develop the first context-aware system (Havard & Podsiad, 2017). Throughout the 1990s, researchers developed additional wearables such as the Pathfinder system, which was the first wearable GPS, as well as prototypes for augmented reality systems (Havard & Podsiad, 2017).

In the early 2000s, the Lilypad Arduino was introduced and began as an academic research project (Buechley & Hill, 2010). "The LilyPad Arduino is a system for experimenting with embedded computation that allows users to build their own soft wearables by sewing fabric-mounted microcontroller, sensor and actuator modules together with conductive thread" (Buechley, Eisenberg, Catchen, & Crockett, 2008, p. 424). The Lilypad project was commercialized in collaboration with Sparkfun Electronics and sold as an e-textile construction kit (Buechley & Hill, 2010). Students in K–12 have used the Lilypad Arduino to make a "touch-sensitive shirt; makes silly sounds when touched in certain places and a police hat that makes siren noises when a switch is pressed" (Buechley & Eisenberg, 2008, p. 14). The Lilypad Arduino serves as the electronic component for many wearable devices.

Although advances in wearable technology have progressed significantly over the past few decades, researchers and educators are continually developing wearable devices and finding new ways to incorporate them into the academic curriculum. Currently, the usage of wearable devices occurs in a variety of ways in K–12 education. Educators and researchers across the globe have infused fitness activity trackers in schools to help students achieve instructional goals. Additionally, wearable technologies may be useful in STEM instruction and educational computing, as

Megan Podsiad,
University of West Florida,
Academic Excellence in Instructional Strategies, 11000 University Parkway, Bldg. 85/126, Pensacola, FL 32514.
E-mail: mpodsiad@uwf.edu

Nancy B. Hastings,
University of West Florida,
Instructional Design and Technology, 11000 University Parkway, Bldg. 85/123, Pensacola, FL 32514.
E-mail: nhastings@uwf.edu

well as a valuable tool to engage students in collaborative learning experiences. Wearable devices are also being used with students to encourage educational gaming and free play. Though there are limitations associated with the use of wearable devices, these technologies have positive implications for teachers and students alike.

WEARABLE FITNESS ACTIVITY TRACKING DEVICES

The introduction of wearables for health-related purposes was not until the 1980s (Price & Rasmussen, 1980). Price and Rasmussen (1980) patented the invention of a wearable heart rate monitor for the wrist that detected and displayed one's pulse rate. The technology has evolved to fitness and activity trackers, smartwatches, and heart-rate monitor chest straps. Wearable technologies are used in K–12 classrooms to engage students in statistics instruction, monitor their physical activity, and motivate them to reach instructional and personal goals.

Wearable activity tracking devices have been used with K–12 students to assist in elementary statistics instruction. Lee, Drake, and Thayne (2016) used Fitbit Ultra and Fitbit One devices during physical education to teach students in Grades 3–8 foundations of statistics and data accuracy. A Fitbit device is a pedometer, or step counter, that uses a "three-axis accelerometer to detect movement" (Lee et al., 2016, p. 357). Steps gathered from the students' activity trackers were used as data to create histograms and provide students with an understanding of variability (Lee et al., 2016). Students created data plots to record trends in activity and used critical thinking skills to analyze differences in individuals' data (Lee et al., 2016). Lee et al. (2015) also used data collected from Fitbit Ultra devices to teach students how to identify measures of central tendency (Lee et al., 2015).

Project GETUP (Gaming to Educate Teens to Understand Personal Health) examined the level of student engagement when tracking one's health using Fitbit One devices (Schaefer, Ching, Breen, & German, 2016). Thirty-four students ages 11 and 12 participated in the study over a 6-month period in an urban middle school afterschool program (Schaefer et al., 2016). Students monitored their weekly activity and synced step data to their personal computer (Schaefer et al., 2016). Schaefer et al. (2016) noted positive changes in physical activity for several students, although some students indicated significant anxiety associated with the wearable technology. Schaefer et al. (2016) also discovered that student engagement declined over time, as students tried to cheat to log more steps. Schaefer et al. (2016) identified several constraints that may have affected the study's outcome. The potential obstacles included limited technology accessibility, design flaws, difficulty using the device, and device loss (Schaefer et al., 2016).

WEARABLE DEVICES AS MOTIVATIONAL TOOLS

Researchers have identified wearable devices as potential motivational tools for K–12 students. Ul Amin, Inayat, and Shazad (2015) analyzed students' interest and motivation to learn with 24 students in the first grade. Ul Amin et al. (2015) programmed smartwatches to contain instructional material such as poems, spelling words, and shapes. The measurement of students' motivation and academic performance were at the end of a 10-week period. Researchers noted that both interest and motivation level increased over the course of the study (ul Amin et al., 2015). According to ul Amin et al. (2015), the "use of the gadget made them excited about their usual course, and they listened to their poems and words, again and again, to memorize them quickly" (p. 3). Additionally, students became motivated to learn about time, due to their interaction with the smartwatch.

The integration of wearable devices into curriculum may impact students' level of intrinsic and extrinsic motivation. De la Guía, Camacho, Orozco-Barbosa, Luján, Penichet, and Pérez (2016) used smartwatches to examine motivation levels in 15 students while learning a foreign language. Smartwatches were used as a tool in a game to locate, identify, and match recipe ingredients (de la Guía et al., 2016). The game helped students practice common vocabulary words and conversational dialog in English (de la Guía et al., 2016). The smartwatches used Bluetooth technology to link with Internet of Things objects and then project objects onto a visualization board (de la Guía et al., 2016). Video cameras were used to observe students while playing the game and a survey was conducted to help determine students' level of intrinsic and extrinsic motivation (de la Guía et al., 2016). Researchers measured indicators of intrinsic motivation including curiosity, explorer collaboration, challenge, and control (de la Guía et al., 2016). Indicators of extrinsic motivation included points, rewards, competitiveness, and comments from the teacher and classmates (de la Guía et al., 2016). De la Guía et al. (2016) concluded although students exhibited characteristics of both intrinsic and extrinsic motivation, intrinsic motivation factors were more visible.

WEARABLES FOR
INSTRUCTIONAL NEEDS

The use of wearable technology to meet instructional goals in the K–12 environment is occurring across the globe. Instructors are incorporating e-textiles and other wearable technology into instruction to improve attitudes and interest in STEM and engineering, as well as educational computing. STEM is the acronym used to "refer to the four separate and distinct fields we know as science, technology, engineering, and/or mathematics" (Sanders, 2009). The United States encourages an integrated STEM curriculum to engage youth in competitive global professions in the fields of technology and engineering (Breiner, Harkness, Johnson, & Koehler, 2012). Lessons that incorporate the engineering design process allow students to connect content knowledge to real-world applications (Riskowski, Todd, Wee, Dark, & Harbor, 2009). Building and programming wearables also encourage creativity and facilitate cooperative learning among K–12 students (Ngai, Chan, Cheung, & Lau, 2009).

Researchers have investigated the influence of wearable technology on the engineering design process (Barker, Melander, Grandgenett, & Nugent, 2015). Researchers who work on the WearTec project at the University of Nebraska investigated the use of e-textiles with students in fourth through sixth grade (Barker et al., 2015). Students used the engineering design process to build e-textiles and also engaged in computing and circuit building (Barker et al., 2015). According to Barker et al. (2015), intermediate students who participate in wearable technology programs have more positive attitudes toward STEM, including motivation to learn, self-efficacy and learning as a whole (Barker et al., 2015). WearTec researchers also found that the use of e-textiles in instruction has been shown to increase interest and participation among female students because it makes engineering and computing personally relevant to them (Barker et al., 2015). Also, Barker et al. (2015) stated the instructional goals of wearable technology are closely related to the goals of the engineering design process; therefore, making the use of these technologies a natural addition to STEM education.

The WearTec project also examined students' ability to conduct basic educational computing skills (Barker et al., 2015). Researchers in this study required students to identify issues with computing and circuitry, as well as troubleshoot possible solutions to computing problems (Barker et al., 2015). Students were required to program the device and master coding to ensure the e-textile would operate properly (Barker et al., 2015). Barker et al. (2015) found e-textiles "allow participants to combine computing technology, circuitry and aesthetics to create projects that are personally meaningful" (p. 73).

Researchers created a flexible, durable e-textile called the TeeBoard that allows students to practice basic educational computing skills (Ngai, Chan, Cheung, & Lau, 2010). Ngai et al. (2010) wanted to develop an e-textile where students may make mistakes that are easily correctable and does not require extensive training or expensive tools (Ngai et al., 2010). Ngai et al. (2010) recognized students in the study would have limited knowledge of educational computing, and therefore, chose the Arduino Lilypad platform because of its feasibility of use. Researchers also developed and utilized the programming system called BrickLayer that students used to program sensors, lights, and buzzers on the TeeBoard (Ngai et al., 2010). During the 5-day workshop, middle school students learned "basic programming concepts such as conditionals, loops, and sequential logic" (p. 49). Programming techniques allowed students to use creativity when developing their TeeBoard, as each group added a unique touch to their e-textile (Ngai et al., 2010).

The TeeBoard project also promoted collaborative learning with K–12 students (Ngai et al., 2009). During a 5-day workshop, 25 students ages 11–16 worked in small groups to assemble and program the TeeBoards (Ngai et al., 2009). Researchers observed several students working on different aspects of one garment at the same time, as they recognized the need to work simultaneously with other students to accomplish instructional goals (Ngai et al., 2009). Students also presented the final e-textile product to other class members at the end of each workshop session (Ngai et al., 2009).

Middle and high school students from different communities collaborated on a wearable project called Engineering Brightness (Fogarty, Winey, Howe, Hancox, & Whyley, 2016). Fogarty et al. (2016) used 3D printers to develop wearable wristwatches with solar-powered lights for children in underdeveloped countries to read at night without electricity (Fogarty et al., 2016). Students from an elementary school in the United Kingdom, a middle school in Colorado and a high school in Canada, worked collaboratively using online conferencing applications, such as Skype (Fogarty et al., 2016). Students shared information about circuits, collaboratively planned and designed the wearable wrist watches, and deepened their understanding of the technology, as well as its philanthropic impacts (Fogarty et al., 2016).

WEARABLES FOR GAMES AND OTHER USES

The incorporation of wearable technology into playtime fosters creativity in young children, encourages physical activity, and allows students to play independently (Rosales, Sayago, & Blat, 2015). Wearable technology has also been piloted in classrooms to assist students with hearing impairments with the use of Google Glass and Quick Response (QR) codes (Parton, 2017).

Wearable technologies serve a valuable purpose for playtime and gaming for young children. The creators of the BeeSim game used e-textile puppets with students ages 7–8 to illustrate how complex systems operate by using honeybees as a participatory simulation (Peppler, Danish, Zaitlen, Glosson, Jacobs, & Phelps, 2010). The first two versions of BeeSim did not use wearable technologies, but instead, focused on the premise of the game (Peppler et al., 2010). The current prototype, BeeSim

Version 3.0, uses LilyPad Arduino as the electronic platform (Peppler et al., 2010). There is a wireless component called the XBee Wireless Module embedded in the students' gloves that allow for seamless communication between the bee puppets and the hive (Peppler et al., 2010). Students used their computational puppets to collect honey and communicate with other students acting as bees, the beehive, and flowers. LED lights situated on the puppet illuminate to notify the student that their computational bee has successfully communicated with other players (Peppler et al., 2010). Students win the game by bringing the most honey to the beehive. However, they also realize the importance of working quickly and communicating with the other bees (Peppler et al., 2010).

Wearable technologies may also be used to facilitate constructionist gaming (Vasudevan, Kafai, & Yang, 2015). Constructionist gaming refers to the process of "making rather than playing your own games for learning" (Vasudevan et al., 2015, para. 1). Vasudevan et al. (2015) analyzed the impact of constructionist gaming on students' level of interest in computing. Researchers facilitated a 4-month-long workshop with 12 middle school students and analyzed students' ability to creatively modify existing games to include wearable controllers (Vasudevan et al., 2015). Students used computational construction to design and create wearable controllers that coincide with the Flappy Birds computer game. Students' wearable controllers were connected to a platform called MaKey MaKey (Vasudevan et al., 2015). MaKey MaKey is an interface that is ideal for beginners and is compatible with almost any software (Silver, Rosenbaum, & Shaw, 2012). Students were encouraged to be creative; therefore, each computational glove looked slightly different and codes varied from student to student (Vasudevan et al., 2015). This workshop provided students with an opportunity to participate in the creation of the controller, as well as the activity of testing and playing with their final product.

Other technologies, such as Wearable Sounds, Statue and FeetUp, are wearable accessories created for use during free play with young children (Rosales et al., 2015). Rosales et al. (2015) piloted three wearable accessories with 24 students enrolled in an after-school program. Students' interactions were examined during playtime while wearing the computational accessories. The Statue is a game that uses a computable belt pouch to monitor students movement (Rosales et al., 2015). The pouch is equipped with "a Lilypad microprocessor, an accelerometer, LEDs, and a piezo speaker" (Rosales et al., 2015, p. 43). Socks called FeetUp uses pressure sensors, LED lights, and sound to encourage movement, as they only chirp when both feet are off the ground (Rosales et al., 2015). Wearable Sounds, or WS, uses a wearable armband that produces sound when in motion (Rosales et al., 2015). While wearing WS, students may select different sounds to be emitted while they move during playtime (Rosales et al., 2015). These three wearable accessories allow students to express themselves creatively through play, sometimes creating new and alternative games to those suggested by the researchers (Rosales et al., 2015).

The use of wearables may also be as assistive technologies for students with hearing or sight impairments. Students with significant hearing impairments may benefit from the development of Glass Vision 3D, which uses a Google Glass application for assistance in the classroom. For this project, Google Glass was used in conjunction with QR codes, allowing students to scan the codes with glasses, prompting an American Sign Language video to appear via augmented reality (Parton, 2017). Parton (2017) piloted this study with fifth-grade students who have hearing impairments. Students can use gestures to access videos on the glasses, rather than use their voice, because many students with hearing impairments are not comfortable with verbal language (Parton, 2017). Parton (2017) found students to be capable and excited about using Google Glass technology in the classroom to make their classroom come to life.

LIMITATIONS

Although the use of wearable technology in the K–12 environment yields positive outcomes in many occasions, researchers and educators have also determined that there are significant concerns to address in the future. Researchers noted that using Google Glass for over 1 hour caused the device to overheat. Therefore, the students had to wait until the glasses were cool before further use (Parton, 2017). Classroom teachers stated that, although wearable technologies sparked interest for their students, instruction took significantly longer than other technologies, such as iPads, even though the outcome was similar (Parton, 2017).

Researchers have also acknowledged that not all schools can afford Fitbits or wearable technologies for students (Lee et al., 2016). Schaefer et al. (2016) noted that it was "difficult to obtain all of the necessary technological resources" (p. 13) to sync wearable fitness devices in their urban afterschool program. Researchers discovered the limitations with school firewalls when uploading Fitbit data to the online website (Lee et al., 2015). Additionally, students may have limited access to the Internet at home to sync wearable device data to online locations (Schaefer et al., 2016). It is possible for school technology specialists to set up temporary accessibility to provide students with online access to their Fitbit data to combat this challenge. Other limitations include privacy and ethical concerns, data storage, and data displays (Lee et al., 2015).

As researchers conduct studies in K–12 settings, they have noted small sample size as a significant barrier in generalizing their findings to a larger population. Barker et al. (2015) stated that because their sample size consisted of only 21 participants in the WearTec study, "the results cannot be generalized to the target population as a whole" (p. 74). These concerns were also echoed by Ngai et al. (2009), who indicated that the sample size of 25 was a limitation of their project. Ngai et al. (2009) stated it is "crucial that it be feasible to run larger-sized workshops" with qualified instructors (p. 56). Additionally, researchers noted that they wished to not only expand their sample size but also with participants of varying age groups. In the Rosales et al. (2015) study, the authors described their desire to test wearable devices with teenagers and adults who they thought "could also benefit from wearables that support their interest in play and social interaction through technology" (p. 47). Regardless of barriers, it is evident that researchers have an overwhelming desire to continue and expand studies of wearable devices for educational purposes.

CONCLUSION AND FUTURE DIRECTIONS

Over time, wearable technologies have continued to advance in both quality and quantity of features offered for consumers, as well as students in K–12 environments (Lindberg, Seo, & Laine, 2016). Researchers and educators alike are creating and presenting wearables that are user-friendly and guide students through basic computing functions (Ngai et al., 2010). With future research, wearables may be easier to incorporate into instruction, allowing both students and teachers the ability to reuse and reprogram interfaces so that they can be modified for other instruction and scaffolded for various concepts in the curriculum (Peppler et al., 2010). Creating wearables such as e-textiles enable students to participate in tactile learning that supports child development and free play (Rosales et al., 2015). Additionally, wearable technologies allow students to learn creatively through the use of STEM disciplines and the engineering design process, which encourages success in higher education (Riskowski et al., 2009).

Future studies may consider training educators in wearable technologies and their implementation to discover how wearables can be incorporated into science, technology, engineering, and mathematics curriculum and instruction (Barker et al., 2015). Limited technology access in some communities may present a challenge when integrating wearables into the K–12 environment (Schaefer et al., 2016). Adapting wearables into education would require a smooth transition by incorporating these technologies a little at a time to avoid a backlash if some technologies do not work as effectively as initially anticipated (Borthwick, Anderson, Finsness, & Foulger, 2015).

It is clear through the various studies discussed above that the analysis of data "captured through wearable technologies and the Internet of Things represents an invaluable source of information" for students and instructors alike (de la Guía et al., 2016, p. 377). Since wearable technologies allow students and teachers to monitor their actions while collecting data, they can look at data from a new, more personal perspective (Lee et al., 2015). Instructional time will essentially be saved in the long run due to quick and efficient data collection using wearables, although additional time may be spent initially learning how to operate these devices (Lee et al., 2015). Based on the current research, students in the K–12 environment are not only benefiting from the use of wearable technologies in the classroom, but they are also open to their use in coordination with other learning tools and strategies (ul Amin et al., 2015).

REFERENCES

Barker, B., Melander, J., Grandgenett, N., & Nugent, G. (2015). Utilizing wearable technologies as a pathway to STEM. In D. Rutledge & D. Slykhuis (Eds.), *Proceedings of SITE 2015—Society for Information Technology & Teacher Education International Conference* (pp. 1770–1776). Las Vegas, NV: Association for the Advancement of Computing in Education. Retrieved from https://www.learntechlib.org/p/150591/

Borthwick, A. C., Anderson, C. L., Finsness, E. S., & Foulger, T. S. (2015). Special article personal wearable technologies in education: Value or villain? *Journal of Digital Learning in Teacher Education, 31*(3), 85–92. doi:10.1080/21532974.2015.1021982

Breiner, J. M., Harkness, S. S., Johnson, C. C., & Koehler, C. M. (2012). What is STEM? A discussion about conceptions of STEM in education and partnerships. *School Science and Mathematics, 112*(1), 3–11. doi:10.1111/j.1949-8594.2011.00109.x

Buechley, L., & Eisenberg, M. (2008). The LilyPad Arduino: Toward wearable engineering for everyone. *IEEE Pervasive Computing, 7*(2), 12–15. doi:10.1109/MPRV.2008.38

Buechley, L., Eisenberg, M., Catchen, J., & Crockett, A. (2008, April). The LilyPad Arduino: using computational textiles to investigate engagement, aesthetics, and diversity in computer science education. In *Proceedings of the SIGCHI conference on human factors in computing systems* (pp. 423–432). doi:10.1145/1357054.1357123

Buechley, L., & Hill, B. M. (2010, August). LilyPad in the wild: how hardware's long tail is supporting new engineering and design communities. In *Proceedings of the 8th ACM Conference on Designing Interactive Systems* (pp. 199–207). doi:10.1145/1858171.1858206

De la Guía, E., Camacho, V. L., Orozco-Barbosa, L., Luján, V. M. B., Penichet, V. M., & Pérez, M. L. (2016). Introducing IoT and wearable technologies into task-based language learning for young children. *IEEE Transactions on Learning Technologies, 9*(4), 366–378. doi:10.1109/TLT.2016.2557333

Fogarty, I., Winey, T., Howe, J., Hancox, G., & Whyley, D. (2016, March). Engineering brightness: Using STEM to brighten hearts and minds. In *Integrated STEM Education Conference (ISEC), 2016 IEEE* (pp. 5–12). IEEE. Retrieved from http://ieeexplore.ieee.org.ezproxy.lib.uwf.edu/stamp/stamp.jsp?tp=&arnumber=7457559

Havard, B., & Podsiad, M. (2017). Wearable computers. In T. Kidd & L. R. Morris, Jr., *Handbook of research on instructional systems and educational technology* (pp. 356–365). Hershey, PA: IGI Global.

Lee, V. R., Drake, J. R., & Thayne, J. L. (2016). Appropriating quantified self technologies to support elementary statistical teaching and learning. *IEEE Transactions on Learning Technologies*, 9(4), 354–365. doi:10.1109/TLT.2016.2597142

Lee, V. R., Drake, J., & Williamson, K. (2015). Let's get physical: K–12 students using wearable devices to obtain and learn about data from physical activities. *TechTrends*, 59(4), 46–53.

Lindberg, R., Seo, J., & Laine, T. H. (2016). Enhancing physical education with exergames and wearable technology. *IEEE Transactions on Learning Technologies*, 9(4), 328–341. doi:10.1109/TLT.2016.2556671

Mann, S. (1997, February). "Smart clothing": Wearable multimedia computing and "personal imaging" to restore the technological balance between people and their environments. In *Proceedings of the fourth ACM international conference on multimedia* (pp. 163–174). doi:10.1145/244130.244184

McCann, J., & Bryson, D. (Eds.). (2009). *Smart clothes and wearable technology*. Cambridge, England: Woodhead.

Ngai, G., Chan, S. C., Cheung, J. C., & Lau, W. W. (2009). The TeeBoard: An education-friendly construction platform for e-textiles and wearable computing. In *Proceedings of the SIGCHI Conference on Human Factors in Computing Systems* (pp. 249–258). doi:10.1145/1518701.1518742

Ngai, G., Chan, S. C., Cheung, J. C., & Lau, W. W. (2010). Deploying a wearable computing platform for computing education. *IEEE Transactions on Learning Technologies*, 3(1), 45–55. doi:10.1109/TLT.2009.49

Parton, B. S. (2017). Glass vision 3D: Digital discovery for the deaf. *TechTrends*, 61(2), 141–146. doi:10.1007/s11528-016-0090-z

Peppler, K., Danish, J., Zaitlen, B., Glosson, D., Jacobs, A., & Phelps, D. (2010, June). BeeSim: Leveraging wearable computers in participatory simulations with young children. In *Proceedings of the 9th International Conference on Interaction Design and Children* (pp. 246–249). doi:10.1145/1810543.1810582

Price, E. G., & Rasmussen, L. C. (1980). *U.S. Patent No. 4,195,642*. Washington, DC: U.S. Patent and Trademark Office.

Riskowski, J. L., Todd, C. D., Wee, B., Dark, M., & Harbor, J. (2009). Exploring the effectiveness of an interdisciplinary water resources engineering module in an eighth grade science course. *International Journal of Engineering Education*, 25(1), 181–195. Retrieved from http://citeseerx.ist.psu.edu/viewdoc/download?doi=10.1.1.580.2126&rep=rep1&type=pdf

Rosales, A., Sayago, S., & Blat, J. (2015). Beeping socks and chirping arm bands: Wearables that foster free play. *Computer*, 48(6), 41–48. doi:10.1109/MC.2015.168

Sanders, M. (2009). STEM, STEM education, STEM mania. *Technology Teacher*, 68(4), 20–26. Retrieved from https://vtechworks.lib.vt.edu/bitstream/handle/10919/51616/STEMmania.pdf?sequence

Silver, J., Rosenbaum, E., & Shaw, D. (2012). Makey Makey: Improvising tangible and nature-based user interfaces. In *Proceedings of the ACM tangible embedded and embodied interaction* (pp. 367–370). Retrieved from https://static1.squarespace.com/static/561c2019e4b0ee65a89cee14/t/580e416615d5db9dfb7c01f2/1477329256087/silver-makeymakey-TEI.pdf

Schaefer, S. E., Ching, C. C., Breen, H., & German, J. B. (2016). Wearing, thinking, and moving: Testing the feasibility of fitness tracking with urban youth. *American Journal of Health Education*, 47(1), 8–16. doi:10.1080/19325037.2015.1111174

Ul Amin, R., Inayat, I., & Shazad, B. (2015, April). Wearable learning technology: A smart way to teach elementary school students. In *12th Learning and Technology Conference, 2015. 35752 2015* (pp. 1–5). doi:10.1109/LT.2015.7587221

Vasudevan, V., Kafai, Y., & Yang, L. (2015). Make, wear, play: Remix designs of wearable controllers for scratch games by middle school youth. In *Proceedings of the 14th International Conference on Interaction Design and Children* (pp. 339–342). doi:10.1145/2771839.2771911

Insights From a Reflective Conversation Among Two Professors and a Student

Instructional Approaches, Accountability, and Building Community in Online Courses

Autumn M. Dodge and Stefanie B. Copp, with Aja Stevens

INTRODUCTION

One only need do a search for online degree programs to reveal the prevalence of distance education in the United States. Institutions offering online degrees have ballooned and are surely not going anywhere anytime soon. According to a report by the Babson Survey Research Group authored by Seaman, Allen, and Seaman (2018), distance learning enrollment increased for the 14th year straight in 2016 and increased steadily

Autumn M. Dodge,
Assistant Professor of Language and Literacy Education, College of Education, Leadership Studies, and Counseling, University of Lynchburg, 1501 Lakeside Drive, 332-H Education Courts, Lynchburg, VA 24501.
Telephone: (434) 544-8715.
E-mail: dodge_am@lynchburg.edu

Stefanie B. Copp,
Assistant Professor of Language and Literacy Education, College of Education, Leadership Studies, and Counseling, University of Lynchburg, 1501 Lakeside Drive, 332-G Education Courts, Lynchburg, VA 24501.
Telephone: (434) 544-8508.
E-mail: copp_s@lynchburg.edu

between 2012 and 2016. This steady increase in distance learning between 2012 and 2016 contrasts with a decline in enrollment in brick-and-mortar institutions in that same time span (Seaman et al., 2018). Ongoing scholarly conversations about distance learning, therefore, are essential. Questions about best practices for teaching in distance learning settings, students' experiences learning online, and ways of harnessing the potential of new technologies continue to emerge, and, likewise, they are relevant topics for discussion and reflection.

Instructors who teach both online and in-person courses can tell you there are overlaps but also major differences between pedagogical approaches in the two modalities. While these differences might seem straightforward, deeper reflection on instructors' pedagogy, their students' learning experiences, and the use of the technology in these two different instructional modalities can provide important insights.

Aja Stevens,
University of Lynchburg,
1501 Lakeside Drive,
Lynchburg, VA 24501.
E-mail: stevens_al@lynchburg.edu

Developing reflective practices is an important goal for all educators to pursue. Notions of reflective practice vary on a continuum, from casual retrospection to following specific frameworks for reflection (Loughran, 2002). Broadly speaking, "reflective practice is understood as the process of learning through and from experience toward gaining new insights of self and/or practice" (Finlay, 2008, p. 1). Dewey's (1938) seminal work on the intricacies of learning from experience provided the foundation for discussions of reflective practice in the field of education. Dewey's ideas were taken up by Schön (1983) as he conceived the *reflective practitioner* (Finlay, 2008, p. 3). While critiques of Schön's work have emerged, his conception of *reflection-in-action* and *reflection-on-action* continue to be a staple in education today.

Finlay (2008) contrasts Schön's two types of reflection. Reflection-in-action is comprised of "professionals ... examining their experiences and responses as they occur" (p. 3). On the other hand, with reflection-on-action "professionals are understood consciously to review, describe, analyse and evaluate their past practice with a view to gaining insight to improve future practice" (Finlay, 2008, p. 3). For both reflection-in-action and reflection-on-action, making connections between thoughts, experiences, and applicable theory are important goals (Finlay, 2008). Loughran (2002) notes that "one element of reflection that is common to many is the notion of a problem (a puzzling, curious, or perplexing situation)" (p. 33). In other words, the first step in reflection is the urge to explore something of particular interest in more depth.

In the field of teacher education, a key goal is to develop in preservice teachers this drive to home in and reflect on problems, puzzles, and curious instances in their own teaching. While there is much literature on developing preservice teachers' reflective practices on their K–12 instruction (e.g., Griffin, 2003; Lee, 2005; Pedro, 2005), literature on joint student-teacher reflection on the pedagogy college/university students experience with their teachers (professors) is less common. In their book *Engaging Students as Partners in Learning and Teaching: A Guide for Faculty*, Cook-Sather, Bovill, and Felten (2014) write about various contexts where such teacher-student reflective practice has taken place. For example, at Bryn Mawr College, a program called Students as Learners and Teachers (SaLT) "pairs undergraduate students with faculty members who wish to analyze and, perhaps, revise their pedagogical approaches over the course of a semester" (Cook-Sather et al., 2014, p. xii). The undergraduate students in these partnerships observe but are not enrolled in the classes of the teacher with whom they are paired because the focus of the SaLT project is reflection on *pedagogy* not content: "the student consultants explore with faculty members classroom dynamics, pedagogical approaches, and the learning experiences of students enrolled in the course" (Cook-Sather et al., 2014, pp. xii–xiii).

The opportunities and outcomes of pedagogical reflection between students and teachers offers unique insights that cannot be reached by teachers reflecting by themselves. This article emerged from a goal Stefanie and Autumn had to engage in such collective reflective practice with a student. Our reflection here differs from the SaLT program in that ours was a one-time reflective session and in that Aja was a student in Stefanie's class. Our reflective session is similar to the SaLT approach in that our reflection focused not on content but on pedagogy (i.e., classroom dynamics, instructional strategies, and students' learning experiences). Unique in our student-teacher reflection is a focus on how these factors operate in the online learning space as well as noting similarities and differences with face-to-face learning spaces.

OUR COLLABORATIVE REFLECTIVE PROJECT

Stefanie and Autumn are both new faculty at our institution and our master's program in reading includes both face-to-face and online classes. Both Stefanie and Autumn have taught online classes in the past but are seeking ways to improve our online pedagogy and incorporate new technologies. Aja is a student who is in her first year in our master's program. She completed her fully face-to-face undergraduate degree at this same institution. The online courses she has taken in our master's program are her first online learning experiences.

Stefanie and Autumn have reflected a lot about our approaches to online teaching and ideas for revising our courses, but we felt that we could get deeper insights about online teaching through hearing a student's perspective. Stefanie had met Aja prior to her joining the program and felt comfortable approaching her to ask if she would be willing to embark on a reflective project about online teaching and learning. At the beginning of the 2018 spring semester, we asked if Aja would keep notes about her experience taking an online class with Stefanie with a plan to reconvene to discuss Stefanie's class near the end of the semester.

In late March of 2018, we gathered via Google Hangouts and had a productive 90-minute discussion about Stefanie's online class. We recorded our discussion so that we could revisit it and reflect further. Stefanie discussed her instructional choices and quandaries; Aja shared her thoughts about Stefanie's comments and offered her critiques, experiences, and insights; I (Autumn) asked questions and looked for parallels or departures from her prior experiences online. She will be teaching online classes in the upcoming year, so this conversation was important to her future planning as well. We transcribed our discussion and returned to reflect on our conversation and pinpoint the most salient ideas.

In what follows, Stefanie and I share what we see as the three most important topics from our conversation with Aja: choosing instructional methods, accountability beyond discussion boards, and building community. To enrich our discussion of these topics, we include excerpts from the transcription of our reflective conversation that capture how we grappled (and continue to grapple) with particular issues. We offer take-aways from our discussion and experiences and pose questions for readers to ponder.

CONVERSATION TOPIC 1: STEFANIE DISCUSSES CHOOSING INSTRUCTIONAL METHODS

As online course offerings have increased, so have the options for delivering information and interacting with each other in the online setting. In many online courses, there is a predictable sequence of activities each week (e.g., readings, discussion boards, online lecture) to ensure that students know what to expect. One tension that I experienced was between replicating my style of teaching in a traditional setting and maintaining consistency to eliminate confusion. For example, one strategy that I often use in the classroom is jigsaw. Jigsaw is a cooperative learning strategy in which students are assigned a "home" group in which each member breaks off to specialize in one aspect of a topic and then returns to the home group to teach them what they learned. I knew this was a powerful learning experience for students in the traditional classroom because of the high level of motivation related to peer accountability. I was able to replicate the jigsaw in an online setting but it required me to provide very clear directions and models prior to the lesson. I used a video describing the strategy and a written explanation to ensure that all of my students were able to participate. When I gave

the directions for the week, I also included a video explaining the jigsaw strategy and a classroom example so they would be able to imagine how this would look in their K–12 classrooms. Further, I offered options for the ways that students would interact. In a traditional classroom, they would meet in small groups, but in this online setting, I was able to allow students to choose to interact via a private discussion board, in a Wiki, or through a Google Hangout meeting. These choices allowed groups to maintain the flexibility that is an appeal of online learning, but also offered opportunities to interact in ways that suited their needs and interests. Likewise, when they presented to their groups they had similar options for presenting. During our conversation, Aja pointed out that doing the jigsaw in a Wiki or discussion board actually provided an increase in the accountability and potentially the rigor of the conversation.

> Aja: I think online you're able to better determine who's doing what, because usually before you post something in Google Docs you're going to put your name beside it when you're typing. But if you're in class you're all sitting together and shouting out information and one person is just typing everything down and no one is like saying well Aja said this, and Dr. [Stefanie] Copp said this, and then you just put it all together and it's not really who did what. So in an online settings it's better for something like that.

Although my teaching style in a face-to-face class is to keep students actively engaged through cooperative learning strategies, there are times that require some level of direct instruction. I struggled with ways you present this type of instruction in an online class. I have seen instructors use video lectures, PowerPoint slides with voice-overs, or simply posting a PowerPoint presentation for students to review. In this course, I tried a range of those methods so this conversation was an opportunity to hear Aja's thoughts about the dissemination of that information.

Aja: I really did like the PowerPoint and Google Slides where you did the voice-over because I could see the bullet points and as I would read them I would get expanded information on them, so I really liked that.

In contrast, we all felt that the use of long video lectures were the least effective methods but short videos such as ones that may precede a class reading may be useful. I created 2-3 minute videos that served as an introduction to the article or chapter and set the purpose for students before they read. We agreed that this type of short burst of information helps keep students focused on the purpose of the week's module.

In considering the use of instructional methods, another challenge that I faced was time management. In a face-to-face course I am able to implement a range of instructional strategies while monitoring the time and adjusting the activity accordingly. In an online format, the activities are assigned at the start of the week and there is little room for adjustment because students are not working in synchrony. During our conversation, I expressed my concern that there were times that I did not provide enough content, while Aja's perception was much different.

Aja: I feel as though the amount of work provided each week during my online courses, with minimal differences, equated to the workload I was given during my face-to-face classes. For example, if I am disciplined and I manage my online workload effectively throughout the course of the week, I am roughly working with the same amount of work I had with my face-to-face classes. Thus, I should be able to get my work done on time.

We concluded that it is a difficult balance and one way that we can help students better manage the load is by clearly explaining the time expectations during the introductory week of the course. It is important that students understand that they should allot the 3 hours for the weekly course content but also plan for time for assignments and any traditional out-of-class time for work to prepare for class or complete assignments. Further, it is ideal for the instructor to check in regularly with students to find out how much time each module is taking and adjust accordingly.

TAKE-AWAY THOUGHTS

We are in a time where online class availability is much more widespread than our knowledge about how to best instruct in an online format. However, issues surrounding the use of particular instructional strategies and time management are prevalent in online and face-to-face courses. It is important for teachers to continue to be willing to try new strategies to best meet the needs of their students. This process also requires reflection on and modification of practices based on those reflections. These are best practices for teachers in all instructional settings, so we should not forget to apply them in an online classroom.

QUESTIONS TO CONSIDER

What are some of the issues that you face in creating online courses? What effective instructional strategies do you use in person that you are also using online? How do you allow for variety in your instructional choices, but also avoid confusion among your students? Which components of your online course can be consistent and where can you introduce variety? How do you gauge the time students will need to spend on each module? How do you help students manage their time so they are not overwhelmed or not committing enough time to get a proper depth of understanding?

CONVERSATION TOPIC 2: AUTUMN DISCUSSES ACCOUNTABILITY BEYOND THE DISCUSSION FORUM

One topic that came up in our discussion was how to create accountability for student participation and engagement in online classes. Accountability for student participation is an essential component of classes and one that can be tricky to parse in face-to-face classes, let alone in online classes. In face-to-face classes, beyond the non-negotiable aspect of attendance, descriptions of requirements for student participation almost always include active engagement in class discussion and any in-class activities. Teachers of face-to-face classes encounter the challenge of assessing the quality of students' engagement. Who is participating in the discussion? Do their contributions to the discussion evidence that they have read the texts and are going beyond the surface level? Are they listening to their classmates in the discussion? Are they taking an active role during small group work?

In online courses, attempts to replicate the discussion routines in face-to-face classes are most often in the form of discussion forums of one sort or another. However, in online classes, how do we capture elements of face-to-face classes *beyond* discussion—the variety of small-group work and activities or other tasks (e.g., asking students to take 8 minutes and draw a mindmap connecting main ideas across texts and then be ready to share out)? And how do these map onto online classes in terms of accountability? In a face-to-face class, these activities are not usually graded—they are just an inherent part of class and sometimes are developed on the spot by the instructor in response to students' needs in the class (e.g., the instructor realizes, based on discussion, that a certain concept needs to be unpacked more).

Stefanie tried out multiple strategies to try to mirror these types of interactions and activities and, similar to small group work and brainstorms in a face-to-face context, she did not grade these activities. One strategy she used was embedded in the PowerPoints she posted each week. At different points throughout her slides, Stefanie would embed a link to a shared Google Doc. Students would click on the link and then respond to questions posed based on the content presented in the slides as well as to each other.

> Aja: I like the links that you provided with the Google Docs. Sometimes I have gone back periodically to see what other people post. The link to the Google Doc made us participate throughout the lesson and made it more engaging...I like the real collaboration between classmates and the Google Doc made sure that we were participating in our work.

Similar to a face-to-face setting where the instructor might stop and ask students to turn to a partner and talk about something for 3 minutes and then return to the discussion, students were not given an explicit grade for their contributions to the Google Doc in Stefanie's online class. Because of this, Stefanie found that, while students like Aja found the Google Doc interaction meaningful, some students simply did not participate. Further, in some of her PowerPoints, students would have to click on the Google Docs or insert comments in order to progress through the PowerPoint. So if students had not done this, Stefanie could see that they had not even listened to the lecture.

> Stefanie: I had the links embedded in the PowerPoint, and once you started the PowerPoint, you couldn't just click on it and go along. There was some level of discussion and accountability because it was apparent to me which students hadn't watched the lecture because they

never commented on the Google Docs. There was nothing posted that said "in this PowerPoint lecture you'll see there are several places where you have to stop and click on it," so they just didn't engage at all.

Stefanie also experimented with using VoiceThread to prompt these types of intermittent contributions among students when they were watching videos. Students could insert VoiceThread recordings at different points in the videos Stefanie posted to comment on the content or pose questions. In our conversation, Aja explained her experience with VoiceThread in Stefanie's class.

> Aja: I really liked VoiceThread. I like being able to comment at specific points in the video. Because if you're commenting after a video but your comment is actually about something at the very beginning, your classmates aren't really going to know exactly what it is that you're talking about. But if you can comment at 59 seconds about something at that point, then your classmates and professor can see that and it's kind of cool to be able to do that.

Despite the enthusiasm about the advantages of VoiceThread expressed by Aja, VoiceThread use was sparse among students in Stefanie's class overall. Stefanie had some students report that they had trouble with the technology. She hypothesized that others, similar to the Google Docs, did not participate because they were not being held accountable by a grade.

During the discussion between Stefanie, Aja, and I, we devoted a good deal of time to grappling with how or whether students should be held accountable for these online equivalents of the in-class small group work and brainstorms found in face-to-face classes that are not individually graded. We discussed the nature of a continuum ranging from completely micromanaging every aspect of online par-

ticipation to expecting that online students should be intrinsically motivated, engaged, and able to self-regulate their online learning. Aja is a highly engaged student who took advantage of the learning opportunities afforded by the embedded Google Docs and VoiceThreads. She and Stefanie compared and contrasted how participation in ungraded activities unfolds with different students.

> Aja: I've always been very passionate about my academics, so I'm going to read all this stuff and make sure to comment and go back to see what everyone's saying because I want to learn about everything.

> Stefanie: I think that's good. For the student like you that's conscientious who's wanting to learn from others, it works. And maybe those are the kind of students who are successful in an online environment—students with intrinsic motivation. Because I can see if a student is just trying to check the box then they're not going to do it…. I just feel like it's micromanaging, which you shouldn't have to do with graduate students.

As with many instructional difficulties, there is not a clear or single reason why students are not participating. It is possible that some students may not participate because they perceive that they already have a strong grasp of a particular concept and do not feel they need the extra practice; however, we concluded through our reflective conversation that if we want all students to participate in these online equivalents of "breakout activities" found in face-to-face courses, then students will have to be held accountable for them.

TAKE-AWAY THOUGHTS

Even if we believe that our online students *should* have the motivation to complete ungraded interactive components in a course, such as writing in embedded Google Docs, posting VoiceThreads while watching a video, we cannot count on them doing so. In a face-to-face class students are held accountable for taking part in things like small group breakout discussions or completing a brainstorm before doing a think-pair-share simply as a function of being present in the room. Including additional interactive components in a online course that are above and beyond discussion forums is surely a best practice, but due to the online format, if we want all students to participate in these activities and be "present" we may have to do more micromanaging in terms of accountability (i.e., grading little interactive components) than we might think (or desire). We need to make it clearer that the expectation is that students participate in *all* of the activities that are posted.

QUESTIONS TO CONSIDER

What degree of intrinsic motivation for interactive engagement between students do you see in your classes? What interactive components beyond discussion forums do you use in your online classes? What technologies have you found most effective for these types of interaction beyond discussion forums? Do you require participation in all of these activities or only some? Should there be some ungraded components of online courses that serve, essentially, as enrichment opportunities for students who are particularly motivated to interact with their online peers and further engage with content?

CONVERSATION TOPIC 3: AUTUMN DISCUSSES THE IMPORTANCE OF BUILDING A LEARNING COMMUNITY

Across learning environments and contexts, building a learning community improves students' learning experiences and outcomes. The teacher plays a significant role in setting the stage for building a learning community, from class configura-

tions (in a face-to-face setting), to the amount of group work, to creating a safe space where students feel comfortable sharing about themselves and their lives. At the core of creating a learning community is *communication* between the teacher and students and between students and their peers. In an online setting, building a learning community can be more of a challenge because the primary mode of communication is in written exchange both between students and between students and their instructor. Technologies such as VoiceThread are great in that students can hear and see each other comment and respond. Obviously, synchronous communication via some video platform is the best way to have communication, but given the asynchronous nature of online courses, this is not always possible and cannot always be required.

The importance of building community was a topic that Aja and Stefanie talked a lot about in our discussion. Aja completed her face-to-face undergraduate education at this institution and is completing this master's program here too. She expressed that it was hard switching from what she could do in terms of working collaboratively with classmates in the face-to-face undergraduate program versus the online courses in our master's program.

> Aja: I will say the hardest thing in this course for me is not having access to classmates, because in undergrad I utilized that—I'd get phone numbers from people and we'd meet up outside of class and if I didn't understand something then we'd not understand it *together* and then reach out to the professor. And with this online class, sometimes it feels weird reaching out in e-mails to someone you don't know, like "Uhhhh this is probably gonna be weird, but hey, I'm in your class." But I *have* met a couple people out of class, like Natalie [pseudonym]. She came into a place I work and said "Hi" and then I was like, "Oooh, you're in my class!" It was really good to put a face to a name.

Stefanie agreed with Aja about the importance of developing these relationships between students. The three of us talked further about how a cohort model in a program has the advantage of having a group of students that move together across courses and can build those relationships that strengthen over time.

> Stefanie: This is definitely a difficulty of not having a cohort, not having a group of friends where you could communicate about your struggles and working through this or talking through that. When you have the relationship established that emerges in cohorts, it makes it easier to navigate the things you're talking about—to e-mail, to collaborate. I think this is a difficulty and so as online educators, if we *don't* have a cohort model, we have to think about what ways can we build that online community.

While Stefanie had made the virtual sessions she offered optional, she expressed that she wants to find more ways to front load virtual sessions early in the semester so that students would be more comfortable reaching out to each other independently to meet virtually.

> Stefanie: I wonder if it would be helpful if there were more opportunities to establish those relationships earlier in the semester through virtual sessions because you would already know your classmates so you'd be willing to get on Google Hangouts and participate later.

While our online classes do not currently require any synchronous virtual sessions (at our institution, online courses are considered asynchronous; synchronous online components cannot be required unless a synchronous requirement is specified in the course listings), Stefanie pondered whether incentivizing such sessions (such as through extra credit) would encourage participation. Aja suggested *changing* the requirements so virtual interaction was built in.

> Aja: I think if there's any assignments in the future where collaboration is required for a group project you should require us to get onto Google Hangouts so we can have that face-to-face interaction and build that rapport.

Making virtual sessions like the voluntary ones that Stefanie held on Wednesday evenings required (as an outcome of this reflective conversation and analysis, Stefanie and I have specified a synchronous component for our program's future online courses in our course listings) would also ensure the establishing of a deep relationship between Stefanie and the students. Stefanie felt that for the students in the class who she had not met on campus or had in another class, it was the voluntary virtual sessions that helped build a relationship with them.

> Stefanie: There are students that I interact with this semester in the virtual sessions that I didn't know or hadn't met before. I feel like they have a deeper connection with me and I have a deeper connection with them because we've interfaced in this way.

TAKE-AWAY THOUGHTS

In Aja's case and for the students in our program, there is the advantage that since our program has both online and face-to-face classes it means that all the people in the classes live in the area. So it is possible for students to get together outside of the online platform if they take the initiative to do so. This is not a reality for all students in online programs. But even in Aja's case in our program, there is a disconnect between students in the class, and even though they live in the same area they do not necessarily feel comfortable reaching out to each other. As instructors in online courses, we need to consider adding required synchronous virtual components to the otherwise asynchronous format. Institutional and/or programmatic constraints as well as the locations of the students (e.g., all in one state, all in the United States, versus in different countries) will impact whether mandatory synchronous sessions are feasible. But as online instructors, we need to actively consider how to encourage as much virtual interaction as possible between students and between students and ourselves in order to create a strong online learning community.

QUESTIONS TO CONSIDER

In what ways do you try to build a strong learning community in your online classes? How do you try to foster strong relationships between students and between students and yourself? Do you require virtual synchronous sessions in your otherwise asynchronous classes? How do students respond to synchronous sessions? Do students seek out opportunities to meet virtually of their own volition or do you need to structure these opportunities? What platforms have you found work best for virtual synchronous meetings?

CLOSING THOUGHTS

As educators, reflecting on our practice and continually aiming to improve and innovate is at the essence of the work we do. The reflection we participated in embodies what Schön coined as reflection-on-action. Together, the three of us made a concrete plan to "consciously to review, describe, analyze and evaluate [our] past practice" (Finlay, 2008, p. 3). In our case, Stefanie focused on her practice, while Aja focused on her experiences and made connections between her experience and Stefanie's pedagogy. Autumn mediated the discussion and posed questions informed by her prior experiences teaching online and her discussions across the semester with Stefanie about her online course. Stefanie and Autumn see our reflection-on-action conversation as a foundation for making informed goals for changes and additions to our online pedagogy and in shaping decisions we make about online courses in our reading program going forward.

In online classes, troubleshooting and improving upon pedagogy sometimes includes more twists, turns, and puzzles than in face-to-face classes. Educators can gain much from reflecting on their own practice as well as pairing with other colleagues to get feedback. However, Stefanie and I found that taking part in shared reflection with a student elevated our reflective practice and provided us with constructive feedback, insights, and recommendations that made us think more deeply about our pedagogy than had Stefanie and Autumn simply reflected together. Further, this kind of in-depth student-teacher reflective conversation allows for a kind of rich dialogic interplay with students about the pedagogy they experience that is simply not possible through the end-of-course evaluations they complete online. Inviting more than one student into such reflective conversations would also allow students to bounce ideas off each other. It could also allow us to see where students' experiences of online learning coincided and diverged. These types of reflective conversations between online students and their teachers can take place via technologies like Google Hangouts, Zoom, Skype, and more. We recommend that other instructors of online classes reach out to students to have these reflective conversations and share their insights with others in the field.

REFERENCES

Cook-Sather, A., Bovill, C., & Felten, P. (2014). *Engaging students as partners in learning and teaching: A guide for faculty.* San Francisco, CA: Wiley.

Dewey, J. (1938). *Experience and education.* New York, NY: Collier.

Finlay, L. (2008). *Reflecting on "reflective practice."* PBPL paper 52, 1–27. Retrieved from http://www.open.ac.uk/opencetl/resources/pbpl-resources/finlay-l-2008-reflecting-reflective-practice-pbpl-paper-52

Griffin, M. L. (2003). Using critical incidents to promote and assess reflective thinking in preservice teachers. *Reflective Practice, 4*(2), 207–220.

Lee, H. J. (2005). Understanding and assessing preservice teachers' reflective thinking. *Teaching and Teacher Education, 21*(6), 699–715.

Loughran, J. J. (2002). Effective reflective practice: In search of meaning in learning about teaching. *Journal of teacher education, 53*(1), 33-43.

Pedro, J. Y. (2005). Reflection in teacher education: exploring pre-service teachers' meanings of reflective practice. *Reflective Practice, 6*(1), 49–66.

Seaman, J. E., Allen, E. I., & Seaman, J. (2018). Grade increase: Tracking distance education in the United States. Retrieved from https://babson.qualtrics.com/jfe/form/SV_djbTFMIjZGYDNVb

Schön, D. A. (1983). *The reflective practitioner: How professionals think in action.* New York, NY: Basic Books.

IN ONLINE CLASSES, TROUBLESHOOTING AND IMPROVING UPON PEDAGOGY SOMETIMES INCLUDES MORE TWISTS, TURNS, AND PUZZLES THAN IN FACE-TO-FACE CLASSES.

PROGRAMS AND DEGREES

UNDERGRADUATE
BACHELOR'S DEGREES
Cardiovascular Sonography (B.S.)*, Fort Lauderdale/Davie Campus
Exercise and Sport Science (B.S.), Fort Lauderdale/Davie Campus
Health Science (B.H.Sc.)**
Medical Sonography (B.S.), Fort Lauderdale/Davie Campus
Respiratory Therapy (B.S.), Palm Beach Campus
Respiratory Therapy (B.S.)**
Speech Language and Communication Disorders (B.S.), Fort Lauderdale/Davie Campus

GRADUATE
MASTER'S DEGREES
Anesthesia (M.S.), Fort Lauderdale/Davie Campus
Anesthesia (M.S.), Tampa Campus
Health Science (M.H.Sc.)**
Occupational Therapy (M.O.T.), Fort Lauderdale/Davie Campus
Physician Assistant (M.M.S.), Fort Lauderdale/Davie Campus
Physician Assistant (M.M.S.), Fort Myers Campus
Physician Assistant (M.M.S.), Jacksonville Campus
Physician Assistant (M.M.S.), Orlando Campus
Speech-Language Pathology (M.S.)‡, Fort Lauderdale/Davie Campus

DOCTORAL DEGREES
Audiology (Au.D.), Fort Lauderdale/Davie Campus
Audiology (Au.D.), United Kingdom
Health Science (D.H.Sc.)**
Health Science (Ph.D.)**
Occupational Therapy (O.T.D.)‡, Tampa Campus
Occupational Therapy (Dr.O.T.)**
Occupational Therapy (Ph.D.)**
Physical Therapy (D.P.T.), Fort Lauderdale/Davie Campus
Physical Therapy (D.P.T.)‡, Tampa Campus
Physical Therapy (D.P.T., transition)**
Physical Therapy (Ph.D.)**
Speech-Language Pathology (SLP.D.)**

healthsciences.nova.edu

*A dual degree B.S. Cardiovascular Sonography/M.H.Sc. program is available at the NSU Tampa Campus.
**Programs are available either completely or partially online.
‡Programs are offered in a hybrid format that combines online and on-campus elements.

Nova Southeastern University admits students of any race, color, sexual orientation, and national or ethnic origin. ■ Nova Southeastern University is accredited by the Southern Association of Colleges and Schools Commission on Colleges to award associate's, baccalaureate, master's, educational specialist, doctorate, and professional degrees. Contact the Commission on Colleges at 1866 Southern Lane, Decatur, Georgia 30033-4097 or call 404-679-4500 for questions about the accreditation of Nova Southeastern University. 08-049-17SAT

Quality Matters

The Implementation of a Quality Assurance Program for a Virtual Campus at a State College in Florida

Rebekah Wright

INTRODUCTION

The demand for online courses and programs continues to rise as more learners are looking for flexible learning options to meet their needs. Despite declining levels seen in overall enrollment, distance education enrollments are steadily growing (Seaman, Allen, & Seaman, 2018). Along with this demand and increase, however, comes a concern of quality among online courses. Quality is conceptually very subjective and there are many ways that quality can be assessed (McCroskey, Kovach, Ding-Miertschin, & O'Neil, 2011). Within higher education, instructors can determine how to assess and evaluate their courses for quality and for improvement. One of the most recognized standardized programs for quality assurance in online education is Quality Matters (McCroskey et al., 2011; Quality Matters, 2016a). The Virtual Campus at Indian River State College implemented the QM standards to assure quality in their online and blended courses. In addition, the Virtual Campus has integrated a master course model design, faculty development and training programs, and several support resources to not only ensure quality for their courses and programs, but also, to promote the overall success of Virtual Campus students.

OVERVIEW OF INDIAN RIVER STATE COLLEGE

Indian River State College (IRSC) is a non-profit, 4-year degree granting institution located on the Treasure Coast in Florida. IRSC has five campus sites in four counties; the Main Campus in St. Lucie County, the Pruitt Campus in St. Lucie County, the Mueller Campus in Indian River County, the Chastain Campus in Martin County, and the Dixon Hendry Campus in Okeechobee County. Governed by the District Board of Trustees, IRSC provides affordable educa-

Rebekah Wright,
Indian River State College,
3209 Virginia Avenue, Fort Pierce, FL 34981.
Telephone: (772) 462-7477.
E-mail: rwright@irsc.edu

tional programing to approximately 29,000 students annually. IRSC offers several degrees and programs including baccalaureate degrees, associate in arts, associate in science, associate in applied science, and a variety of technical certificate and adult education programs (Indian River State College, 2010a). Due to the increasing need for more flexible learning options, IRSC launched an advanced center to deliver web-based educational content and programs to its student population.

ACCREDITATION

According to the IRSC (2010b) website, "Indian River State College is accredited by the Southern Association of Colleges and Schools Commission on Colleges" (para. 5). Additionally, IRSC has program specific accreditations including the commission on dental accreditation for the dental hygiene program, the commission on accreditation of allied health education programs for the emergency medical services program, the commission on accreditation for health informatics and information management education, the commission on accreditation of allied health education programs, the national accrediting agency for clinical laboratory sciences, the accreditation commission for education in nursing, the commission on accreditation in physical therapy education, the joint review committee on education in radiologic technology, and the commission on accreditation for respiratory care (IRSC, 2010b).

MISSION AND GOALS

IRSC is committed to "creating a superior teaching and learning environment, cultivating student success, embracing diversity, stimulating economic growth, developing a highly skilled workforce, building partnerships to expand opportunities, and providing cultural enrichment and lifelong learning" (IRSC, 2010c, para. 1).

The mission of IRSC is fulfilled through the following goals:

- student access and success.
- fiscal resources.
- student development and satisfaction.
- physical resources.
- educational programs.
- workforce development.
- cultural diversity.
- economic development.
- technology.
- employee development (IRSC, 2010c, para. 1)

INDIAN RIVER STATE COLLEGE VIRTUAL CAMPUS

The IRSC Virtual Campus was created in 2013 and currently "serves as the central agent for online learning" at the institution (About IRSC, 2010a, para. 2). The virtual campus seeks to meet the needs of the ever-changing student population as well as overcoming the many challenges associated with rapidly advancing technologies. Their goal is "to be leaders in the application of new, leading-edge technologies for learning (Virtual Campus, 2010a, para. 3).

LEADERSHIP

According to Simonson, Smaldino, and Zvacek (2015), institutions that engage in distance education should have the proper administrative personnel who is qualified to lead and direct the distance education operations within the institution. The IRSC Virtual Campus falls under the direct leadership of the vice president of institutional technology and the assistant dean of the virtual campus (see Figure 1). Since its inception, the IRSC Virtual Campus has expanded its leadership professionals to include 19 key personnel: a dean, a director, five instructional designers, three course developers, two project coordinators, two e-Learning technologists, and five video production specialists (A.

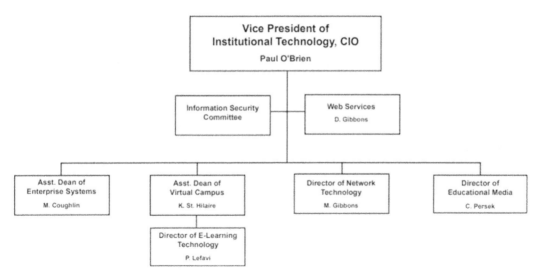

Figure 1. Indian River State College organizational chart, 2017–2018.

Moore, personal communication, April 5, 2018). The collaborative efforts of these stakeholders have allowed the virtual campus to expand, offering more distance education resources and opportunities to enrolled students.

Virtual Campus Courses and Degree Programs

Allen and Seaman (2017) reported that the pattern of growth for distance education has continued to rise and that the higher education sector has seen about a 4% increase from the previous year. Additionally, approximately 30% of learners enrolled in higher education courses are taking at least one online course. In order to respond to this increase, the Virtual Campus at IRSC offers several affordable and flexible options for learners. There is a total of 12-degree programs that learners can complete entirely online. These programs include:

- associate in arts degree;
- associate in science degree in business administration;
- associate in science degree in computer information technology;
- associate in science degree in health information technology;
- bachelor's degree in business administration;
- bachelor's degree in criminal justice;
- bachelor's degree in exceptional student education/esol endorsement;
- bachelor's degree in information technology management/cyber security;
- bachelor's degree in middle grades mathematics education;
- bachelor's degree in nursing;
- bachelor's degree in organizational management;
- bachelor's degree in public administration (with concentrations in emergency planning and management and public policy and leadership).

In addition to the 12 online degree programs, the IRSC Virtual Campus offers over 100 courses that can be completed entirely online (Virtual Campus, 2010d).

Technology Requirements for Online Learning

The computer requirements for virtual campus students include an Internet browser such as Microsoft Internet Explorer, Firefox, Chrome, or Safari, as well as plug in requirements including Java for file uploads and Adobe Flash for webcam recordings and video viewing. Many of the features and functionality of the BlackBoard Learning Management System (LMS) require additional plugins. Additionally, online learners are encouraged to download the BlackBoard mobile learn app so that course content can be accessed from anywhere at any time with a mobile device (Virtual Campus, 2010b).

COURSE DESIGN PROCESS

The virtual campus at Indian River State College uses two models to design and develop their online courses. The ADDIE model and the master course model. The ADDIE model is one of the traditional models for instructional design and is the foundation for many other instructional design models (Reiser & Dempsey, 2012). The ADDIE model is used as a systematic approach to instructional design. The five phases of the ADDIE model are analysis, design, development, implementation, and evaluation (Reiser & Dempsey, 2012). The virtual campus utilizes the ADDIE model in their course design process to ensure that the design of online courses is both systematic and effective.

The master course model is a concept in where instructional designers, course developers, and subject matter experts's collaborate to design a master course. This course can be replicated into multiple sections and taught by multiple instructors, reliably and continually (Hill, 2012). The virtual campus utilizes a master course model and collaborates with members of the virtual campus team to create storyboards and instructional materials. A master course model allows the virtual campus to produce courses that are consistent, have an organized structure, and appearance (A. Moore, personal communication, April 5, 2018). The master course model

serves as a template and design model for virtual campus courses therefore the layout for course components is always consistent.

LEARNING MANAGEMENT SYSTEM

Virtual Campus courses and degree programs are delivered through the Blackboard learning management system (see Figure 2). Learning management systems are designed for the effective delivery of educational content, typically in the form of full courses. Using a learning management system allows the virtual campus to meet the needs of online students by creating a properly designed distance education environment.

The Blackboard LMS allows virtual campus students to interact with each other and the system asynchronously from various geographic locations (Reiser & Dempsey, 2012). All courses at IRSC require either instructor or student interaction with the Blackboard LMS. Hence, IRSC's online, blended, and face to face courses integrate the LMS within the design of the courses in order to support formal and cooperative learning as well as promote consistency, reliability, and quality among all courses, regardless of delivery method.

QUALITY MATTERS

In 2003, a consortium of professionals dedicated to online education, called MarylandOnline, Inc. sought to create a process in which online courses would be of the same quality regardless of educational content (Quality Matters, 2016a). From this the Quality Matters or QM Program was formed. With the help of the Fund for the Improvement of Postsecondary Education grant, a grant for the improvement of postsecondary education, Quality Matters was able to develop a standardized rubric and a peer review process that can be replicated among all institu-

Figure 2. IRSC Blackboard Student Login Screen.

tions nationwide (Lowenthal & Hodges, 2015). Now a nationally recognized certifying organization, Quality Matters has over 60,000 subscribing members.

Quality Matters is a faculty-centered peer review process that is based on the Community of Inquiry Framework. The community of inquiry framework has been used to conceptualize community in the context of the online environment, specifically, online discussions (deNoyelles, Zydney & Chen, 2014). According to Garrison, Anderson, and Archer (2000), the community of inquiry framework has three elements that contribute to a successful educational experience; social presence, cognitive presence, and teaching presence. As a part of the course design process, the Virtual Campus at IRSC utilizes the QM rubric to ensure course quality, equivalency, and consistency.

The QM Rubric

The QM rubric is an evaluative tool used to assess online programs and courses. It can also be used as a model for effective course design (Simonson et al., 2015). In 2012, the virtual campus integrated the QM rubric as a part of the course design process (A. Moore, personal communication, April 5, 2018). The QM rubric consists of eight general standards and 43 specific review standards to be incorporated as a way to ensure course quality and consistency. The eight general standards are:

1. course overview and introduction;
2. learning objectives;
3. assessment and measurement;
4. instructional materials;
5. course activities and learner interaction;
6. course technology;
7. learner support; and
8. accessibility and usability (Lowenthal & Hodges, 2015, p. 86).

The QM rubric should be used by instructional designers and course developers to create courses based on the standards at the onset of the design process. The rubric is also used as a course assessment tool when evaluating if a course meets the standards and in what areas the course can be improved (Quality Matters, 2016b).

QM COURSES

All courses that are a part of a virtual campus degree program are nationally certified through QM. By using a consistent design and format, virtual campus students are able to focus on course content and actively learning. The virtual campus has dedicated a significant amount of time and financial resources in order to properly integrate the QM standards into virtual campus courses (A. Moore, personal communications, April 5, 2018). The virtual campus hopes that the integration of the QM rubric will lead to better alignment between course objectives, activities, and assessments.

BEST PRACTICES FOR ONLINE TEACHING

The virtual campus has created best practices for online teaching and learning aligned with the QM standards. The best practices are stated as:

1. Etiquette expectations—also known as netiquette. These are expectations that guide instructors in explaining how learners are to communicate in the course.
2. Response time and feedback—faculty at IRSC are encouraged to keep learners engaged by providing substantial feedback in a timely manner. The instructor is responsible for providing the learner with information regarding feedback and response times in the course syllabus.
3. Minimum technology requirements—faculty should clearly list the technology requirements that learners will be required to obtain and utilize throughout the course.
4. Minimum technical skills—students need a variety of technical skills to be successful in online courses. Some of these skills include properly using the LMS, downloading and installing software, using spreadsheets, word processing, and presentation programs.
5. Course grading—assessments are a critical indicator of student success. Instructors are encouraged to clearly describe the grading policies and how grades are calculated (Virtual Campus, 2010).

PEER REVIEW PROCESS

All virtual campus courses that are QM certified must go through an internal and external peer review process (see Figure 3).

Virtual campus instructors are required to complete the QM training and peer review certification program. To become a certified peer reviewer, instructors must take the Applying the QM Rubric workshop and the Peer Reviewer Course. The virtual campus course at IRSC are reviewed internally by faculty members who are QM certified and approximately 20% of the virtual campus courses are sent to be externally reviewed and certified by QM (A. Moore, personal communication, April 5, 2018). After a course is submitted for external review, a team of peer reviewers will evaluate the course against the standards and provide feedback. The course has to meet the standards at 85% quality level or better to receive certification (Quality Matters, 2016c).

FACULTY DEVELOPMENT

The qualifications that the virtual campus faculty hold is critical to their success as online instructors. Institutions should have guidelines to direct the instructional practices of online instructors and they can aid faculty in improving online instructional practices by offering training and technological resources (Simonson et al., 2015). The IRSC Virtual Campus offers technology training as well as virtual campus instructor training courses to improve the success of online faculty members. Virtual Campus faculty, as well as other institutional faculty, are provided a variety of professional development opportunities throughout the academic year. Additional professional development opportunities

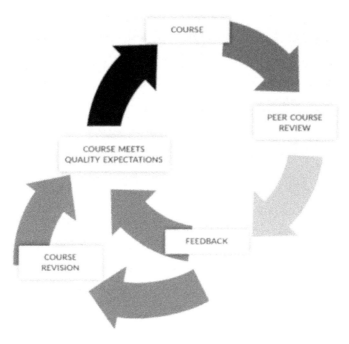

Figure 3. QM peer review process.

are available for faculty members through the Institute for Academic Excellence. The Institute for Academic Excellence is a center for faculty exploration, inquiry, and reflection. The institute collaborates with the employee development program and the Virtual Campus to provide opportunities for faculty to pursue excellence in instructional pedagogy and learning (Institute for Academic Excellence, 2010). There are many challenges that exist for instructors who are developing courses and teaching in an online environment (Walters, Grover, Turner & Alexander, 2017). Designing meaningful professional development programs for virtual campus instructors allows for improvements in instructor satisfaction as they transition from traditional course delivery methods to distance education.

Virtual Campus Instructor Training (VCIT)

The virtual campus offers a training and professional development course for any faculty or staff member who is considering online instruction. The Virtual Campus Instructor Training (VCIT) course includes the following topics: online pedagogy, best practices, plagiarism, netiquette, online behavior, and LMS fundamentals (Virtual Campus, 2010c). The VCIT course provides an opportunity for online instructors to further their knowledge as online instructors and participate in a collaborative learning experience with other instructors who are transitioning into the online environment.

Technology Training

As technology continues to rapidly advance, the training needs of online faculty members at the virtual campus broaden. In order to address these needs, the virtual campus and the institute for academic excellence offers technology training opportunities for faculty. The trainers assist with one on one trainings, as well as, technology centered workshops and open labs. Faculty are provided resources and trainings in several areas including Echo360, BlackBoard Collaborate, BlackBoard instructional video series, grade center training, as well as assistance with Web 2.0 tools and presentation tools such as smart boards, Prezi, Camtasia, Weebly, Microsoft Office applications, and the green screen for video production (Virtual Campus, 2010c).

STUDENT RETENTION AND SUCCESS

The virtual campus at IRSC is committed to student retention and student success. The virtual campus provides numerous resources to support online students and reduce some of the barriers experienced by distance education learners. By providing these resources, online students are better equipped to meet the demands of online education. Some of the resources provided by the virtual campus to learners include a student success guide, virtual campus information sessions in each semester, BlackBoard LMS support guides, videos, and tutorials (Virtual Campus, 2010e). In addition, there are several virtual campus initiatives that are currently underway to help support students including a new online proctoring service for distance learners, the Complete Florida initiative, and an Open Educational Resource initiative. The OER initiative was started in 2016 as a response to the increasing cost of textbooks. The virtual campus, faculty members, and librarians are investing in this initiative in hopes that the cost savings and open access to course materials will show eventual improvements in success rates.

CONCLUSION

In order to address the needs of distance education students, the Virtual Campus at IRSC has taken steps to not only ensure that Virtual Campus courses are of good quality, but also that they are consistent and highly organized. By aligning online

courses with the QM rubric and designing them using a Master Course Model, the Virtual Campus is able to deliver their online courses and degree programs to distance education students in a more structured and reliable way. The Virtual Campus at IRSC hopes that this rigorous course design combined with the skills and expertise of certified online faculty, will ultimately improve student success and retention at the institution.

REFERENCES

Allen, I. E., & Seaman, J. (2017). *Digital learning compass: Distance education enrollment report 2017*. Retrieved from https://onlinelearningsurvey.com/reports/digtiallearningcompassenrollment2017.pdf

deNoyelles, A., Zydney, J. M., & Chen, B. (2014). Strategies for creating a community of inquiry through online asynchronous discussions. *Merlot Journal of Online Learning and Teaching, 10*(1), 153–165.

Garrison, D. R., Anderson, T., & Archer, W. (2000). Critical inquiry in a text-based environment: Computer conferencing in higher education. *The Internet and Higher Education, 2*(2–3), 87–105.

Hill, P. (2012). Online educational delivery models: A descriptive view. EDUCAUSE Review 47(6). Retrieved from https://er.educause.edu/articles/2012/11/online-educational-delivery-models--a-descriptive-view

Indian River State College. (2010a). *About IRSC*. Retrieved from http://www.irsc.edu/aboutirsc/aboutirsc.aspx

Indian River State College. (2010b). *Accreditation*. Retrieved from http://www.irsc.edu/aboutirsc/aboutirsc.aspx?id=449

Indian River State College. (2010c). *Indian River State College Mission Statement & College Goals*. Retrieved from https://www.irsc.edu/aboutirsc/aboutirsc.aspx?id=447

Institute for Academic Excellence. (2010). *About us*. Retrieved from http://www.irsc.edu/IAE/IAE.aspx?id=4294972596

Lowenthal, P., & Hodges, C. (2015). In search of quality: Using quality matters to analyze the quality of massive, open, online courses (MOOCs). *International Review of Research in Open and Distance Learning, 16*(5). Retrieved from http://search.proquest.com.ezproxylocal.library.nova.edu/docview/1754596268?accountid=6579

McCroskey, S., Kovach, J. V., Ding, X., Miertschin, S., & O'Neil, S. L. (2011). Quality assurance in e-learning. In S. B. Eom & J. B. Arbaugh (Eds.), *Student satisfaction and learning outcomes in e-learning: An introduction to empirical research* (pp. 231–248). Hershey, PA: IGI Global.

Quality Matters. (2016a). *About*. Retrieved from https://www.qualitymatters.org/about

Quality Matters. (2016b). *Course design rubric standards*. Retrieved from https://www.qualitymatters.org/qa-resources/rubric-standards/higher-ed-rubric

Quality Matters. (2016c). *Process*. Retrieved from https://www.qualitymatters.org/why-quality-matters/process

Reiser, R. A., & Dempsey, J. V. (2012). *Trends and issues in instructional design and technology* (3rd ed.). Boston, MA: Allyn & Bacon.

Seaman, J. E., Allen, I. E., & Seaman, J. (2018). Grade increase: Tracking distance education in the United States. Retrieved from https://onlinelearningsurvey.com/reports/gradeincrease.pdf

Simonson, M., Smaldino, S., & Zvacek, S. (2015). *Teaching and learning at a distance Foundations of distance education* (6th ed.). Charlotte, NC: Information Age.

Virtual Campus. (2010a). *About the virtual campus*. Retrieved from http://virtualcampus.irsc.edu/about.html

Virtual Campus. (2010b). *Best practices for online teaching and learning*. Retrieved from http://virtualcampusfacultysupport.weebly.com/best-practices.html

Virtual Campus. (2010c). *Virtual campus faculty resources*. Retrieved from http://virtualcampusfacultysupport.weebly.com/

Virtual Campus. (2010d). *Online programs*. Retrieved from http://virtualcampus.irsc.edu/online-programs.html

Virtual Campus. (2010e). Information session dates and resources. Retrieved from http://virtualcampus.irsc.edu/orientation--resources.html

Walters, S., Grover, K. S., Turner, R. C., & Alexander, J. C. (2017). Faculty perceptions related to teaching online: A starting point for designing faculty development initiatives. *Turkish Online Journal of Distance Education, 18*(4), 16. Retrieved from http://search.proquest.com.ezproxylocal.library.nova.edu/docview/2011265344?accountid=6579

THE VIRTUAL CAMPUS HOPES THAT ITS RIGOROUS COURSE DESIGN COMBINED WITH THE SKILLS AND EXPERTISE OF CERTIFIED ONLINE FACULTY WILL ULTIMATELY IMPROVE STUDENT SUCCESS AND RETENTION.

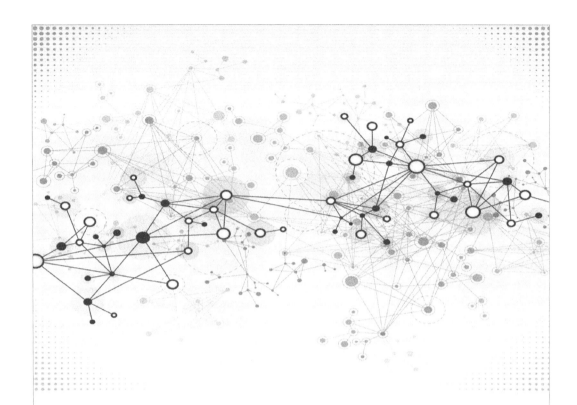

TEACHING AND LEARNING AT A DISTANCE

Foundations of Distance Education

SIXTH EDITION

Michael Simonson

Sharon Smaldino

Susan Zvacek

Get Your Copy Today—Information Age Publishing

Google Classroom for the Online Classroom

An Assessment

Myra Cook Brown

INTRODUCTION

In K–12 and higher education settings alike, pure face-to-face courses are becoming less common. As digital technology's role in education rises and hybrid and online courses become the norm, educators look for online delivery methods that are both cutting edge and cost effective. By the same token, educators need online delivery methods to be workable. Educators are experts in their chosen fields, and they are teachers. But they are not always technocrats. As Grady

Myra Cook Brown,
Academic Advisor,
Utah State University,
356 W 280 N,
Logan, UT 84322.
E-mail: cookmyra@gmail.com

and Davis point out (2005), online courses, in particular, can require a steep technological learning curve, as the instructor develops the entire online learning environment. "Teaching online requires course designers to implement a much more rigorous instructional design process than is required for face-to-face instruction" (p. 108).

To complicate the matter further, it is a given that not all technologies are equal. Therefore, with the growing array of available products, all educators, but especially online educators, need reliable reviews of technologies. Further, even the best technologies are not suited to every educational environment. Consequently, educators need reviews that speak to the applicability of a product to their teaching needs.

One educational technology that is worth a look is Google's G-Suite for Education (GS-E). Google has invested a great deal in GS-E and publicizes it as a full-fledged member of Google's family of suites. Released in 2016 as a part of Google's G-Suite family, GS-E integrates all of Google's previous education products, Google Apps for Education, into one system (Google, 2016a). As Google points out, this cohesive suite of products can scale. Indeed, GS-E has features that can support one class, multiple classes taught by one instructor, or larger administrative units such as schools and school systems (Google, 2016b). GS-E comprises Classroom, which acts as the course hub, while the entire suite of other Google products such as Docs, Calendar, Sheets, Hangouts, Chat, and Gmail, support and amplify Google Classroom, as needed. As one review puts it, "Classroom is, in essence, the service that ties all of Google's tools together for teachers" (TechCrunch, 2017). This flexibility allows GS-E to be used to different degrees. Given the publicity surrounding this product, it is worth considering as an online teaching tool.

To assess GS-E's merits as a tool for an online course, I created a module for an introductory online technical communication course. Creating a course module provides a representative experience in course design, which, in turn, can be scaled to include an entire course. Further, because Google Classroom sits at the center of the suite and the other Google tools are pulled into it as needed, using Classroom to create a course module can serve as good litmus test for the entire suite.

GETTING STARTED

This product is free to educators, and there are no advertisements. Additionally, both instructors and learners have unlimited data storage. It should be noted that while this is indeed generous, it also assumes that many learners will get "hooked into the Google ecosystem and cloud storage services" and become lifelong habitués (TechCrunch, 2014).

Google products tend to have their own look and feel. With 1.2 billion active Google accounts (DMR Stats and Gadgets, 2017), Google's ubiquitousness makes it likely that many instructors and learners have had some exposure to Google products. Further, Google Classroom is intuitive. Indeed, after "playing" with this product for an hour, I felt very comfortable with it. The steps for getting started are exactly what one would expect when creating any new project, big or small. Therefore, there is not a steep learning curve to get the ball rolling.

USING GOOGLE CLASSROOM TO CREATE AN ONLINE COURSE

Not only is Classroom easy to get up and running, its uncomplicated design makes it easy to use to create a course. Classroom has three parts or tabs (see Figure 1): ABOUT, STUDENTS, and STREAM. That's it. In the next sections, I review the functionality of these tabs.

THE ABOUT TAB

I found using the ABOUT tab to be very straightforward. One key feature of interest to online instructors is the way course materials are added to Classroom. As the portal for adding materials to Classroom, ABOUT opens to a menu of storage venues. Along with selecting files from the computer's hard drive and Google Drive, users can search for files using Recent and Starred options, which are timesavers. Further, it is drag-and-drop, so no uploading is required. This is a very fluid, easy-to-use system, which is very helpful for a busy online instructor.

Additionally, the ABOUT tab houses the Classroom Calendar, which includes assignment due dates and times, as well as course announcements. Classroom Calendar automatically syncs with created assignments and announcements. Whatever the format of a course, a strong, clear calendaring system is essential. This is particularly so in an online setting. While Classroom already has due dates on the assignment descriptions themselves, Classroom Calendar reinforces those dates clearly. Figure 2 provides a screenshot of Classroom Calendar.

THE STUDENTS TAB

Like the ABOUT tab, the STUDENTS tab set up is easy to grasp, and it has some time-saving features for instructors. Student information is easy to see and track. One vital functionality that Classroom handles well is how grading and commenting on

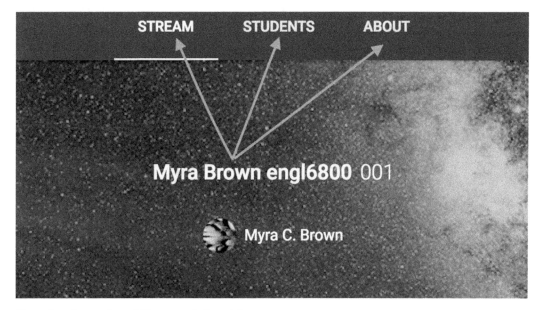

Figure 1. Screenshot of Classroom's three tabs.

Figure 2. Screenshot of Google Calendar.

student work is done. The STUDENTS tab allows instructors to open any submitted assignment within a student's account, correct and comment on it, and assign a grade. Everything happens within the system, so, again, no downloading and uploading are required. Besides supporting Google products, such as Docs and Charts, the system supports Microsoft office, and some Adobe products, including PDFs.

THE STREAM TAB

Up to this point, I have given Classroom a favorable review as a viable product for an online course. Like the other two tabs, the STREAM tab has much to offer online instructors. Unfortunately, the STREAM tab disappoints in a key area.

Let's start with the positives. I found the STREAM tab to be straightforward. Its uncomplicated, almost aerodynamic design makes figuring out functionality painless. Aptly named, STREAM is the course stream. STREAM supports the same products that STUDENT does, so users do not need to tailor their preferences to it.

With the exception of Classroom Calendar, the features of the other two tabs are for instructor use and view only. STREAM, on the other hand, is what students see. This is where students access pretty much everything to do with the course, including assignment descriptions, and supporting materials. Discussions take place here, too. STREAM is chronological, so course modules, assignments, and the like, move through time, an important unifying property of any course. As Fielding's (2016) research suggests, "[Online students] sense that they are moving through time together," and this journey together can bolster a learning community (p. 109). Important information such as assignment titles and due dates are posted clearly, making it very readable. Figure 3 is a screenshot illustrating STREAM's chronological set up and readability.

Now for the negatives. The characteristic that makes Classroom so doable can almost be viewed as STREAM's undoing. STREAM's nonfussy, streamlined design means there are few components. On the other hand, by its nature, an online course requires the entire structure of the course be present on the course site (Grady & Davis, 2005). Such a complex, multifaceted endeavor needs a multifaceted tool. Of particular importance to an online course is the course overview or syllabus. As Grady and Davis (2005) point out, a "syllabus [provides] the framework or scaffolding for the entire course" (p. 109).

STREAM's design lacks a natural, intuitive place for a course overview or syllabus. A course overview needs to be easily accessible, and visibly separate from the chronological flow of the course. STREAM does not provide this. Certainly, an instructor can create a course overview and post it to STREAM. However, because STREAM holds only chronological items, the course overview is merely one of many chronological items. It does not hold pride of place, thus weakening its stabilizing role. One workaround might be to make the syllabus the first post and reference it specifically in the title of each module or assignment. Additionally, because Classroom as a whole is well organized, an instructor might initially post the syllabus to STREAM; then, rely on the flow of the class to hold things together. Obviously, these are not ideal solutions.

Of specific concern is the potential for a diminished teaching presence, as defined by constructivist pedagogical theory. Garrison (2007) notes that "teaching presence is a significant determinate of student satisfaction, perceived learning, and sense of community" in an online learning community (p. 67). Garrison further observes that while "interaction and discourse" are key components to higher order learning, higher order learning also requires "structure (design) and leadership (facilitation and direction)," in other words, teaching presence (p. 67). A visible, standalone course overview can significantly contribute to the structure and leadership that feed into teaching presence.

I would not say that Classroom's inability to handle a course overview or syllabus well is a deal breaker for online instruction, but it is perilously close to being one. Before rejecting GS-E out of hand, one would need to weigh its cost (nothing) and what it does deliver against what it does not deliver. The fact that GS-E is free is not trivial, and it has some wonderful features. Are those factors enough?

Delivery Platforms

The last feature I review is delivery platforms. GS-E delivers well to the range of devices out there. It scales smoothly to phones, tablets, laptops, and desktops. Androids, iPhones, PCs, Macs: they all

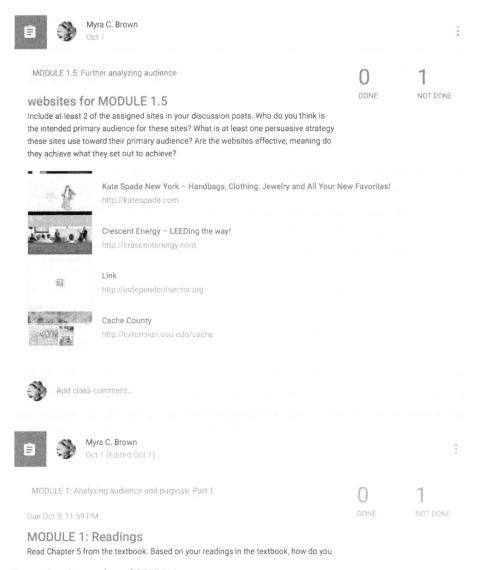

Figure 3. Screenshot of STREAM.

work equally well. Additionally, it does not prefer Chrome over other web browsers.

Future Directions for Inquiry

This paper addresses Classroom from the instructor's perspective. A similar paper from the learner's perspective would be informative.

Conclusion

Google has thrown its entire weight behind GS-E, and it shows. This is a well-thought-out, elegantly designed product. Its inherent structure allows for more features to be easily added down the road. Further, Google offers this suite to schools at no cost. This product can scale to large and small educational courses and systems. Unfortunately, its streamlined design limits creating a visible, centralized course overview or syllabus. This missing functionality is problematic for online instruction. Instructors can create workarounds to compensate, but doing so is less than ideal. Online instructors and administrators considering implementing GS-E would need to carefully weigh the pros and cons.

REFERENCES

DMR Stats and Gadgets. (2017). 18 amazing Gmail statistics and facts. Retrieved from https://expandedramblings.com/index.php/gmail-statistics/#.WdGofBNSxyo

Fielding, H. (2016). "Any time, any place": The myth of universal access and the semiprivate space of online education. *Computers and Composition, 40*, 103–114.

Garrison, D. R. (2007). Online community of inquiry review: Social, cognitive, and teaching presence issues. *Journal of Asynchronous Learning Networks, 11*(1) 61–72.

Google. (2016a). Google for education. Retrieved from https://edu.google.com/?modal_active=none

Google. (2016b). Higher ed solutions. Retrieved from https://edu.google.com/higher-ed-solutions/g-suite/?modal_active=none

Grady, H. M., & Davis, M. T. (2005). Teaching well online with instructional and procedural scaffolding. In K. Cargile Cook & K. Grant-Davie (Eds.), *Online education: Global questions, local answers* (pp. 101–122). Amityville, NY: Baywood.

TechCrunch. (2014). Google launches drive for education with unlimited storage. Retrieved from https://techcrunch.com/2014/09/30/google-launches-drive-for-educationwith-unlimited-storage/

TechCrunch. (2017). Google says its G Suite for Education now has 70M users. Retrieved from https://techcrunch.com/2017/01/24/google-says-its-g-suite-for-education-now-has-70m-users/

TEACHING ONLINE REQUIRES COURSE DESIGNERS TO IMPLEMENT A MUCH MORE RIGOROUS INSTRUCTIONAL DESIGN PROCESS THAN IS REQUIRED FOR FACE-TO-FACE INSTRUCTION.

A Comprehensive Model for Evaluating E-Learning Systems Success

Dimah Al-Fraihat, Mike Joy, and Jane Sinclair

INTRODUCTION

Education is one of the fields that has improved rapidly as a direct result for the development of information and communications technology (ICT), and stimulated to adopt e-learning. E-learning directly resulted from the integration of education and technology and is increasingly considered a powerful medium for learning.

E-learning has facilitated learning by delivering a learner-centered and interactive learning environment to anyone, anywhere, and anytime (Khan, 2005). In addition, it plays a significant role in shifting from teacher-centered to student-centered education (Taha, 2014, p. 2).

Despite e-learning's successful implementation, a considerable number of e-learning projects fail to achieve their goals, and face slow progress and increasing dropout rate (Frimpon, 2012; Liaw, 2008). In addition, evaluating the success of e-learning systems is still an issue facing e-learning stakeholders.

A significant number of studies have focused on the issue of e-learning success. In fact, they fulfil the needs of e-learning

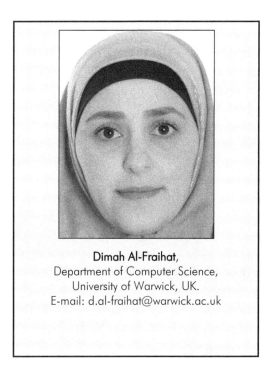

Dimah Al-Fraihat,
Department of Computer Science,
University of Warwick, UK.
E-mail: d.al-fraihat@warwick.ac.uk

Mike Joy,
Department of Computer Science,
University of Warwick, UK.
E-mail: M.S.Joy@warwick.ac.uk

stakeholders to a certain extent but do not meet all of the requirements. There remain disagreements about the factors that are most influential in measuring e-learning systems' success. This direction of research has received little attention for developing an overarching model that can assess e-learning systems' success from different perspectives.

This study aims to fill this void by proposing a comprehensive model for evaluating the success of e-learning. The significance of this study is in identifying the determinant factors and constructs impacting the success of e-learning systems and group these factors in a model that is believed to be holistic because different perspectives are considered in developing the model.

EVALUATING THE SUCCESS OF E-LEARNING SYSTEMS

E-learning systems are multidisciplinary systems, for which consensus on their definition has not been achieved (Al Sabaway, 2011; Lee, Choi, & Kang, 2009; Ozkan & Koseler, 2009). Many researchers have evaluated e-learning systems from computer science, information systems, psychology, pedagogy, and technology perspectives.

Various methods, frameworks, and models have been introduced to measure e-learning systems' success. The contributions to evaluating e-learning systems' success can be categorized into four such approaches: technology acceptance model (TAM); the DeLone and McLean IS success model (D&M); user satisfaction models; and e-learning quality models.

TECHNOLOGY ACCEPTANCE MODEL (TAM)

TAM is a widely used model in the information system field. It was developed first in 1989 (Figure 1) to measure the success of a new technology in terms of the acceptance and use of this technology. The model presumes that there are factors that impact the users' decisions when they face a new technology.

In the context of e-learning, many studies adopted TAM to evaluate the success of e-learning in the same manner as information systems success (Hayashi, Chen, Ryan, & Wu, 2004; Lee, Choi, et al., 2009; Liaw, 2001; Limayem & Cheung, 2008; Martins & Kellermanns, 2004; McFarland, 2001; Ngai, Poon, & Chan, 2007; Ong & Lai, 2006; Roca, Chiu, & Martínez, 2006; Sánchez & Hueros, 2010; Selim, 2003, 2007; Stoel & Lee, 2003; Wang & Chiu, 2011; Yi & Hwang, 2003). These studies vary between validating and testing the robustness of the model by providing empirical evidence on the existing relationships between model factors, to studies that have changed the model's constructs and extended it to include factors applicable in the context of e-learning.

From the studies found in the literature, it is evident that TAM is a commonly used model. TAM has been adopted and/or extended to include other factors that

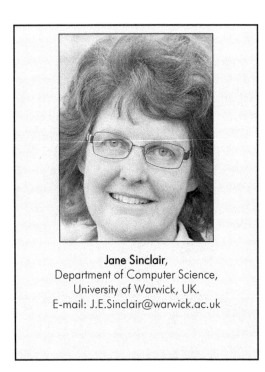

Jane Sinclair,
Department of Computer Science,
University of Warwick, UK.
E-mail: J.E.Sinclair@warwick.ac.uk

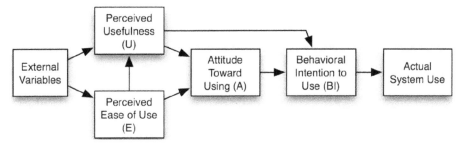

Figure 1. TAM model (Davis, 1989).

influence the acceptance of e-learning. It is concluded from previous research that some factors are more outstanding than others and have a significant impact on the acceptance of e-learning systems, for example, self-efficacy, while others need more investigation, for instance, habit, gender, and perceived resources.

THE DELONE AND MCLEAN IS SUCCESS MODEL (D&M)

The D&M model is a common model that has been used for measuring the success of information systems. It has been extensively cited in academic papers, and reportedly used in over 300 (Delone & McLean, 2003). The D&M model is one of the most important models in information systems. It first appeared in 1992 and was updated in 2003 to include six constructs (Figure 2): system quality, information quality, service quality, use, user satisfaction, and net benefit.

The D&M model was applicable in the field of e-learning in the same manner (Adeyinka & Mutula, 2010; Almarashded, Noraidah, Azan, & Mukhtar, 2010; Hassanzadeh, Kanaani, & Elahi, 2012; Holsapple & Lee-Post, 2006; Hsieh & Cho, 2011; Klobas & McGill, 2010; Lee & Lee, 2008; Lin & Lee, 2006; Lin, 2007, 2008; Masrek, Jamaludin, & Mukhtar, 2010; Wang & Wang, 2009). The validity of the model has been tested by measuring the success of e-learning as a whole or partially and others have extended this model by including other factors that influence the success of e-learning. Other researchers have combined the model with other models and theories to explore widely the factors affecting the success of e-learning systems (Al Sabawy et al., 2011).

The D&M model has been successfully used for measuring the success of different e-learning systems and most of the studies empirically demonstrated its validity and reliability.

USER SATISFACTION MODELS

The user satisfaction approach has been used widely by researchers in the field of e-learning (Kang & Lee, 2010; Leclercq, 2007; Ong & Lai, 2007; Pike Tayles & Abu Mansor, 2010). Sun, Tsai, Finger, Chen, & Yeh (2008) developed a six-construct model to measure e-learning based on learner, instructor, course, technology, design, and environment (Figure 3). The results of the study revealed that learner computer anxiety, instructor attitude toward e-learning, e-learning course flexibility, e-learning course quality, perceived usefulness, perceived ease of use, and diversity in assessments are the critical factors affecting learners' perceived satisfaction (Sun et al., 2008).

Ozkan and Koseler (2009) assessed the user's satisfaction with learning management system (LMS) and proposed a multidimensional model via six dimensions (Figure 4): system quality, information quality, service quality, supportive factors, learner perspective, and instructor attitudes.

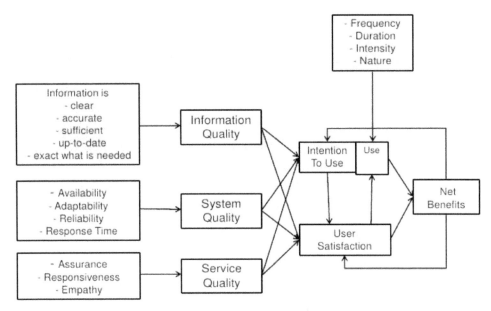

Figure 2. Delone and McLean (2003) model of information systems success.

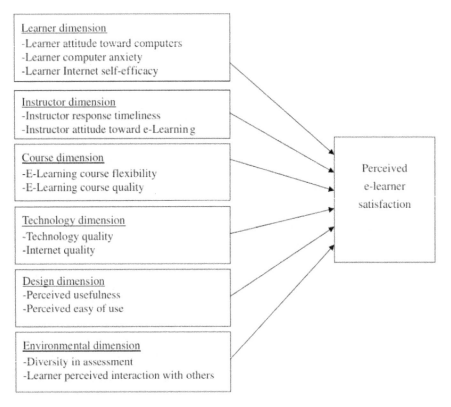

Figure 3. Satisfaction model (Sun et al., 2008).

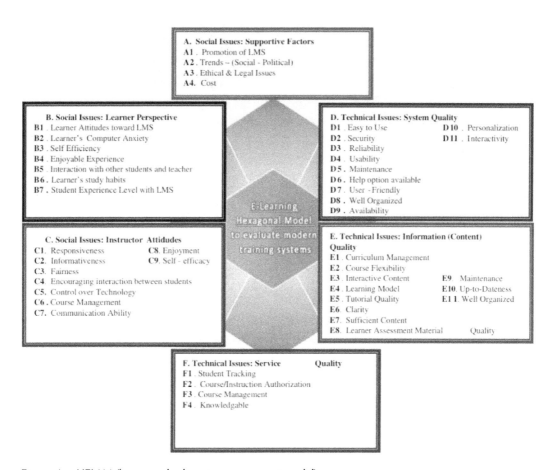

Figure 4. HELAM (hexagonal e-learning assessment model).

In 2010, Naveh, Tubin, and Pliskin conducted a study to investigate students' use and satisfaction of LMS and the relation between these two factors and organizational factors. According to this study, use and satisfaction are significantly correlated with organizational variables: course content and size, instructor status, and the existence of interactive functionalities like forum showed significant correlation with LMS use. The study also reveals low correlation between course discipline and satisfaction.

E-LEARNING QUALITY MODELS

Different approaches and models have emerged to assess the overall quality of e-learning, for example, MacDonald, Stodel, Farres, Breithaupt, & Gabriel's (2001) demand-driven learning model (DDLM) (Figure 5).

The demand-driven learning model was developed to evaluate the benefits of web-based learning. It has five main components: the quality standard of "superior structure," three consumer demands (content, delivery, and service), and learner outcomes (MacDonald et al., 2001).

Another approach to measure the quality of e-learning was introduced by Ehler (2004) based on the learner's perspective. This study was developed to identify the critical indicators adopted by learners to evaluate the quality of e-learning. The study identified seven main constructs used by learners for assessing the quality

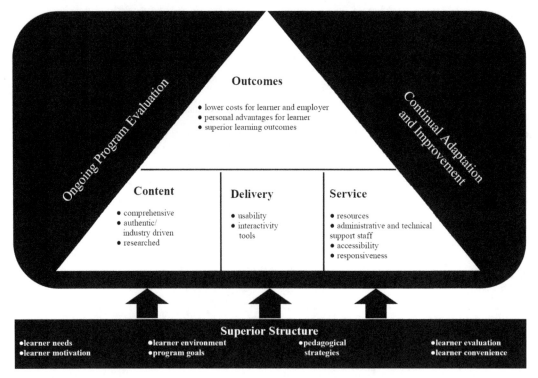

Figure 5. Demand-driven learning model (Macdonald et al., 2001).

of e-learning: tutor support, cooperation and communication in the course, technology, cost-expectations-value, information transparency, course structure, and didactics.

In 2007, Ehlers provide a new model for e-learning quality based on the participation of educational stakeholders. The model identified four dimensions of quality: knowledge, experience, innovation, and analysis.

Pawlowski, Barker, and Okamoto (2007) presented ISO/IEC 19796-1 and compared it with existing approaches of e-learning quality. Abdellatief, Sultan, Jabar, and Abdullah (2011) proposed a model for e-learning quality based on developer's view with four main measurement indicators service content, system functionality, information technology and system reliability and proposed 11 subcharacteristics with its attributes by following the structure of standard IOS/IEC 912.

Considerable research has focused on measuring e-learning quality and proposing models and indicators for this purpose. However, the complexity and generality of the "quality" concept is an issue encountered by researchers. In addition, the varied e-learning stakeholders put more pressure to identify the measurements most suitable for each group.

METHODOLOGY

In order to develop a model for evaluating the success of e-learning systems, we used the constructs of the four models: (D&M) model; TAM; User Satisfaction Models; and E-learning Quality Models. In spite of all their strengths, the four models still have defects (Hassanzadeh et al., 2012), they partially fulfil the needs of e-learning success assessment, and they need to be customized for e-learning areas. In addition, there is still room for improvements and extensions (Marangunic & Granic, 2013). In this article, to propose a more comprehensive model, a synthesis of these previous models is presented.

CONCEPTUAL MODEL

Based on the results and analysis of the literature review, a conceptual model is proposed. The model is believed to be comprehensive for measuring the success of e-learning system. The model is based on six perspectives: quality; usefulness; satisfaction; user attitude; social factors; and benefits of using the system.

The selection of the model constructs is based on the four approaches for evaluating the success of e-learning: DeLone and McLean, TAM, Satisfaction, and Quality approaches and based on their importance in measuring the success of e-learning systems field.

APPROACH 1:
DELONE AND MCLEAN MODEL

In order to build a model for evaluating e-learning systems success we used, first, the D&M model measurements. Because this model was developed to measure information systems success and these systems have no pedagogy theme, it has to be customized for the e-learning area.

The technical quality is another important determinant of the quality of e-learning, and technical problems strongly influence the overall success and satisfaction of users. On the other hand, students are very concerned about the quality of the information (course content) to be clear, easily understandable, appropriate breadth, and has up-to-date content. As a result, a more customized version, to meet the specific needs of the students, is needed.

So we incorporated the Quality construct with four measures (Technical System Quality, Pedagogical System Quality, Information Content, and Service Quality).

The System Quality was decomposed into two factors, technical and pedagogical system quality, as suggested by Hassanzadeh et al. (2012) and Ozkan and Koseler (2009) to be appropriate in the context of e-learning.

Technical System Quality is related to technical success of the issues related to the system (DeLone & McLean, 2003) and measured by the indicators in Table 1.

Pedagogical System Quality consists of the quality measures according to the educational functionalities and capabilities that facilitate teaching and learning (Lee 2010; Hassanzadeh et al., 2012), for example, existence of features like chats and forums that facilitate interactivity and communication with other students and instructors. The Table 2 summarized the pedagogical system quality factors.

Information Quality (Content) is the measure of system semantic success (Delone & McLean, 2003) that is related to the quality of the output (Wang & Wang, 2009) (see Table 3).

The last theme in the Quality construct is *Service Quality*. The quality of the service delivered through electronic media has received noteworthy attention in the context of e-learning (Al Sabawy, 2012). Four indicators were employed to gauge service delivery quality in e-learning (see Table 4).

Benefits of using the system, in a restricted sense, is the impact of using the e-learning system on an individual or group. This construct assesses the different benefits obtained from using the system. In a broader sense it is the benefit to the organization and community as a whole. For the purposes of developing our model, only benefits of using the system on individuals are considered with three determinants: achieving goals; system loyalty; learning benefits. The broader benefits of using the e-learning systems are beyond the scope of the present study, so it was excluded. Indicators of the benefits construct supported by related studies are presented.

TABLE 1

1.	Ease of use	DeLone and McLean (2003); Hasanzadeh et al. (2012); Ozkan and Koseler (2009); Sun et al. (2008); Shee and Wang (2008); Wang and Lio (2008); Holsapple and Lee-Post (2006); Wang, Wang, and Shee (2007); AbuSneineh and Zairi (2010)
2.	Ease of access	DeLone and McLean (2003); Holsapple and Lee-Post (2006); Hasanzadeh et al. (2012); Ozkan and Koseler (2009); Wang et al. (2007); Volery and Lord (2000)
3.	User friendliness	Shee and Wang (2008); Hasanzadeh et al. (2012); Holsapple and Lee-Post (2006)
4.	Reliability	DeLone and McLean (2003); Shee and Wang (2008); Holsapple and Lee-Post (2006); Hasanzadeh et al. (2012); Ozkan and Koseler (2009); Lin and Lee (2006); Volery and Lord (2000); Selim, (2007); Fresen, (2007); Bhuasiri, Xaymoungkhoun, Rho, and Ciganek (2012)
5.	Security	DeLone and McLean, (2003); Hasanzadeh et al. (2012); Ozkan and Koseler (2009); Holsapple and Lee-Post (2006)
6.	Personalization	DeLone and McLean (2003); Ssemugabi and De Villiers (2007); Piccoli, Ahmad, and Ives (2001); Shee and Wang (2008); Hasanzadeh et al. (2012); Ozkan and Koseler (2009); Wang et al. (2007)

TABLE 2

1.	Interactivity	Hasanzadeh et al. (2012); Ozkan and Koseler (2009); Lee (2010); Lim, Lee, and Nam (2007); Pituch and Lee (2006); Holsapple and Lee-Post (2006); Basak, Wotto, and Bélanger (2016)
2.	Learning styles	AbuSneineh and Zairi (2010); Fresen (2007); Bhuasiri et al. (2012); Khan (2005); Fetaji and Fetaji (2009)
3.	Assessment material	Fresen (2007); Cheawjindakarn et al. (2013); Zaiane (2002); Fetaji and Fetaji (2009); Phipps and Merisotis (2000); Basak et al. (2016); Khan (2005)

TABLE 3

1.	Well-organized content	Holsapple and Lee-Post (2006); Roca et al. (2006); Wang et al. (2007); Ozkan and Koseler (2009); Wang and Wang (2009); Ramayah, Ahmad, and Lo (2010); Volery and Lord (2000)
2.	Sufficient content	DeLone and McLean (2003); Holsapple and Lee-Post (2006); Bolliger, Supanakorn, and Boggs (2010); Ozkan and Koseler (2009); Ho and Dzeng (2010); Wang et al. (2007); Lin (2007); Oztekin, Kong, and Uysal (2010)
3.	Clarity	Ozkan and Koseler (2009); Holsapple and Lee-Post (2006)
4.	Up-to-date content	Lin, (2007); Ozkan and Koseler (2009); Holsapple and Lee-Post (2006); Shee and Wang (2008); Wang and Liao (2008); Wang et al. (2007)

TABLE 4

1.	Promptness	Holsapple and Lee Post (2006); Lin (2007)
2.	Responsiveness	DeLone and McLean 2003; Holsapple and Lee-Post (2006); Ozkan and Koseler (2009); Wang et al. (2007); Lin (2007); Sun et al. (2008)
3.	Fairness	Ozkan & Koseler (2009); Levy (2007); Wang et al. (2007)
4.	Knowledge	Lin, (2007); Ozkan & Koseler (2009); Holsapple and Lee-Post (2006); Shee and Wang (2008); Wang and Liao (2008); Wang et al. (2007)

Achieving Goals is one of the components that has a significant role in measuring the success of e-learning and has to be included in our model. It measures the acquisition of skills that influence achieving the personal goals and improving the academic development of students (see Table 5).

System Loyalty is another factor included in our model, which is related to students' involvement and dependence on the e-learning systems (see Table 6) (Hassanzadeh et al., 2012; Lin & Lee, 2006).

Learning Benefits are used to measure the student's performance improvement resulting from using the e-learning system and other benefits of learning in terms of saving students' time in searching for the information and course materials (see Table 7).

APPROACH 2: TAM

In respect to TAM, ease of use, perceived usefulness, and use are considered the major constructs in this model. The evidence presented by previous studies support the selection of the three con-structs to measure e-learning system success. Consequently, it was included in this model.

Ease of Use was defined, according to Davis (1989), as "the degree to which an individual perceives using the e-learning system free of effort" (p. 319). In the e-learning era prior researchers adopted "ease of use" as a central determinate of student satisfaction and the success of e-learning systems. Indicators for ease of use are shown in Table 8.

Perceived Usefulness is a construct employed in this model to predict different factors. It was defined as "The degree to which a person believes that using a particular system would enhance his or her job performance" (Davis, 1989, p. 319). Empirical research has showed the reliability of this construct as a predictor of intention to use. Davis (1989), Joo, Lim, and Kim. (2011), Drennan, Kennedy, and Pisarski (2005), and Hsieh and Cho (2011) found that perceived usefulness had the strongest effect on student satisfaction among the factors that predicted this construct.

TABLE 5

1.	Individual achieving personal goals	Hassanzadeh et al. (2012); Law and Lee (2010); Lin (2008); Antonis, Daradoumis, Papadakis, and Simos (2011); AbuSneineh and Zairi (2010); Fresen (2007); Liaw (2008); Islam (2013); Law and Lee (2010); Lee and Lee (2008)
2.	Academic performance	

TABLE 6

1.	Dependence on the system	Wang and Liao (2008); Wang et al. (2007); Hassanzadeh et al. (2012); Hsiu-Fen Lin (2008); Lin and Lee (2006); Duan, He, Feng, Li, and Fu (2010); Holsapple and Lee-Post (2006); Lee (2010); Lin (2007)
2.	Return to use the system	
3.	Suggest to others to use the system	

TABLE 7

1.	Improve learning process	Lin (2008); Wang et al. (2007); Parker and Martin (2010); Ho and Dzeng (2010); Wang and Liao (2008); Duan et al. (2010); Sørum (2012)
2.	Save time	
3.	Systematically manage the learning process	

Table 9 shows the determinants used to gauge this construct.

Intention to Use is an attitude toward using the system (Davis, 1989; DeLone & McLean, 2003) and is defined as the users' decision to use the system before actually doing so (Hassanzadeh et al., 2012). Table 10 lists details of some studies that targeted identifying the intention to use in the context of e-learning.

APPROACH 3: SATISFACTION

User Satisfaction is a fundamental measurement in the success and acceptance of technology. Several studies considered satisfaction as a single construct to evaluate the success of an e-learning system (DeLone & McLean, 2003) or as multiple constructs; (Sun et al., 2008; Ozkan & Koseler, 2009). It was found that user satisfaction is a valuable learner's attitude construct to incorporate in our model that was validated and supported by several studies (see Table 11).

Social Factors have been considered an important construct in measuring the success of e-learning. Ozkan and Koseler (2009) considered e-learning systems as a sociotechnical entities and the success of e-learning as a combination of "social issues" and "technical issues" and other circum-

TABLE 8

1.	Interaction is clear and understandable	Davis (1989); Hong, Thong, Tam (2006); Islam (2011); Yi and Hwang (2003); Selim (2003); Ngai et al. (2007); Limayem and Cheung (2008); Lee et al. (2009); Wang and Chiu (2011); Gong and Yu (2004)
2.	Interaction does not require a lot of mental effort	
3.	Ease in finding the information you want to	
4.	Overall, it is easy to use it	

TABLE 9

1.	Using the model is of benefit to the student	Davis (1989); Limayem and Cheung (2007); (2006); Islam (2011); Toral, Barrero, and Martínez-Torres (2007); Roca et al. (2006); Martinez-Torres et al. (2008); Gong and Yu (2004)
2.	The advantages outweigh the disadvantages	
3.	Overall the system is advantageous	

TABLE 10

1.	Belief that use of the system is worthwhile	Davis (1989); Lin (2008); Selim (2007); Hassanzadeh et al. (2012); Roca et al. (2006); Gong and Yu (2004).
2.	Tendency to use the system	

TABLE 11

1.	Satisfaction with system performance	DeLone and McLean (2003); Wang et al. (2007); Wu, Tennyson, Hsia, and Liao (2010); Holsapple and Lee-Post (2006); Lee (2010); Bolliger et al. (2010); Sun et al. (2008); Ozkan and Koseler (2009); Chen and Jang (2010); Oztekin et al. (2010)
2.	Users being pleased with system	

TABLE 12

	Learners' Perspective	
1.	Attitude toward e-learning	Selim (2007); Ozkan and Koseler (2009); Roca et al. (2006); Law and Lee (2010); Chen and Yeh (2008); Liaw et al. (2007); Piccoli et al. (2001); Ozkan and Koseler (2009)
2.	Computer anxiety	Bowdish, Chauvin, and Vigh (1998); Piccoli et al. (2001); Zaharias and Poulymenakou (2003); Hayashi, Chen, Ryan, and Wu (2004); Webster and Hackley (1997); Sun et al. (2008); Ozkan and Koseler (2009)
3.	Self-efficacy	Ozkan and Koseler (2009); Picolli et al. (2001); Zaharias and Poulymenakou (2003); Granic (2008); Hiltz and Johnson (1990); Sun et al. (2008)
4.	Experience with e-learning	Ozkan and Koseler (2009); Rosenberg (2006)

TABLE 13

	Instructors' Perspective	
1.	Attitude toward e-learning	Sun et al. (2008); Ozkan and Koseler (2009)
2.	Responsiveness	Sun et al. (2008); Ozkan and Koseler (2009)
3.	Encouraging interaction between students	Liu and Cheng (2008); Wu et al. (2008); Ssemugabi and Villiers (2007); Ozkan and Koseler (2009)
4.	Teaching style	Selim (2007)
5.	Control over technology	Volery and Lord (2000); Webster and Hackley (1997)
6.	Course management	Dillon and Gunawardena (1995)
7.	Communication ability	Picolli et al. (2001); Levy (2007)

stances. Previous research supported e-learning as social entity being an important indicator for successful systems (Liaw et al., 2007; Selim, 2007; Wang et al., 2007). The technical part in our model is covered in the quality construct adopted from the DeLone and McLean model. Accordingly, social factors with three major determinants (learners, instructors, and supportive issues) are added to our model (see Tables 12 and 13).

APPROACH 4: QUALITY MODELS

As mentioned earlier in this article, quality of e-learning is a complicated concept and metrics for measuring the quality of e-learning are diverse based on different perspectives of different stakeholders. A significant contribution to measure the quality of e-learning, which has been presented by several researchers and has been tested and confirmed in studies, are the supportive issues which are incorporated in our model as "support factors" under social factors construct based on the model proposed by Ozkan and Koseler (2009) (see Table 14).

Another important factor presented under the fourth approach is *Academic Performance*, which was employed in the Lee and Lee (2008) model. Academic performance is included in our model under the Benefits as suggested by (Hassanzadeh et al., 2012; Lee & Lee, 2008).

PROPOSED MODEL

According to previous studies on e-learning and the performed analysis, the

TABLE 14

	Support Factors	
1.	Access to library materials	Selim (2007); Khan (2005); AbuSneineh and Zairi (2010); Govindasamy (2001); Oliver (2001); Antonis et al. (2011); Fetaji and Fetaji (2009); Cheawjindakarn et al. (2013)
2.	Support from technicians	
3.	Support from university	
4.	Infrastructure availability	
5.	Ethical-legal issues	

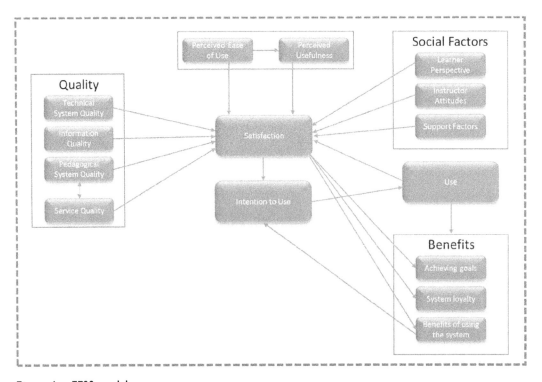

Figure 6. EESS model.

constructs, factors, and relations between model constructs were identified. As a result, a model for evaluating the e-learning systems success EESS is presented (Figure 6).

CONCLUSION AND FUTURE RESEARCH DIRECTION

This study has proposed a model for evaluating e-learning systems success (EESS) encompassing a collective set of measures associated with e-learning systems. In this article, we have proposed a comprehensive model based on different perspectives in relation to quality, usefulness, social factors, user satisfaction, attitude, and benefits of using the e-learning systems. However, several researchers confirmed, "the success of e-learning is a multidimensional and interdependent construct" (Delone & McLean, 2003) and it is essential to examine the interrelationships between these constructs (Hassanzadeh et al., 2012; Ozkan & Koseler, 2009) in more detail. Therefore, future research efforts will be conducted to focus on and test the relationships between the proposed model constructs within the context of e-learning. Another future endeavor will be to check the validity of the model on learning management systems.

The EESS model is not a fixed and unchanged model and is subject to further and continuous developments. Future research may extend this model through adding the organizational perspective and other indicators to cope with the continuous development and changes in the e-learning field. In this regards, the EESS model is composed of the major constructs and factors which are basics for successful evaluation of e-learning. In conclusion, 52 measures grouped under 7 constructs for measuring the success of e-learning systems will be of great benefit to those involved in e-learning as a guidance to gain a better understanding of the issues related to evaluating the success of e-learning systems.

REFERENCES

Abdellatief, M., Sultan, A. B., Jabar, M., & Abdullah, R. (2011). A technique for quality evaluation of e-learning from developers perspective. *American Journal of Economics and Business Administration, 3*(1), 157–164.

AbuSneineh, W., & Zairi, M. (2010). An evaluation framework for e-learning effectiveness in the Arab world. In P. Peterson, E. Baker, & B. McGaw (Eds.), *International Encyclopedia of Education* (pp. 521–535). Oxford, England: Elsevier.

Adeyinka, T., & Mutula, S. (2010). A proposed model for evaluating the success of WebCT course content management system. *Computers in Human Behavior, 26*(6), 1795–1805.

Almarashded, I. A., Noraidah, S., Nor Azan, M. Z., & Mukhtar, S. A. (2010). The success of learning management system among distance learners in Malaysian university. *Journal of Theoretical and Applied Information Technology 21*(2), 80–91.

Al Sabawy, A. Y., Cater-Steel, A., & Soar, J. (2011, July). Measuring e-learning system success

(Research in progress). In *Proceedings of the 15th Pacific Asia Conference on Information Systems* (PACIS 2011) (pp. 1–15). Brisbane, Queensland, Australia: Queensland University of Technology.

Antonis, K., Daradoumis, T., Papadakis, S., & Simos, C. (2011). Evaluation of the effectiveness of a web-based learning design for adult computer science courses. *IEEE Transactions on Education, 54*(3), 374–380.

Basak, S. K., Wotto, M., & Bélanger, P. (2016). A framework on the critical success factors of e-learning implementation in higher education: A review of the literature. *World Academy of Science, Engineering and Technology, International Journal of Social, Behavioural, Educational, Economic, Business and Industrial Engineering, 10*(7), 2335–2340.

Bhuasiri, W., Xaymoungkhoun, O., Zo, H., Rho, J. J., & Ciganek, A. P. (2012). Critical success factors for e-learning in developing countries: A comparative analysis between ICT experts and faculty. *Computers & Education, 58*, 843–855.

Bolliger, D. U., Supanakorn, S., & Boggs, C. (2010). Impact of podcasting on student motivation in the online learning environment. *Computers & Education, 55*(2), 714–722.

Bowdish, B., Chauvin, S., & Vigh, S. (1998, April). *Comparing student learning outcomes in hypermedia and analogue assisted lectures.* Paper presented at the annual meeting of the American Educational Research Association, San Diego, CA.

Cheawjindakarn, B., Suwannatthachote, P., & Theeraroungchaisri, A. (2012). Critical success factors for online distance learning in higher education: A review of the literature. *Creative Education, 3*(8), 61.

Davis, F. D. (1989). Perceived usefulness, perceived ease of use, and user acceptance of information technology. *MIS quarterly, 13*(3), 319–340.

DeLone, W. H., & McLean, E. R. (2003). The DeLone and McLean model of information system success: A ten-year update. *Journal of Management Information Systems 19*(4), 9–30.

Drennan, J., Kennedy, J., & Pisarski, A. (2005). Factors affecting student attitudes toward flexible online learning in management education. *The Journal of Educational Research, 98*(6), 331–338.

Duan, Y., He, Q., Feng, W., Li, D., & Fu, Z. (2010). A study on e-learning take-up intention from an innovation adoption perspective: A case in China. *Computers & Education, 55*(1), 237–246.

Ehlers, U. D. (2004). Quality in e-learning. The learners perspective. *European Journal of Open, Distance and E-Learning, Article 101,* 1–7.

Ehlers, U. D. (2007). Quality literacy: Competencies for quality development in education and e-learning. *Educational Technology and Society, 10*(2), 96–108.

Fetaji, B., & Fetaji, M. (2009). E-learning indicators: A multi-dimensional model for planning and evaluating e-learning software solutions. *Electronic Journal of e-Learning, 7*(1), 1–28.

Fresen, J. (2007). A taxonomy of factors to promote quality web-supported learning. *International Journal on ELearning, 6*(3), 351.

Frimpon, M. F. (2012). A re-structuring of the critical success factors for e-learning deployment. *American International Journal of Contemporary Research, 2*(3), 115–127.

Gong, M., Xu, Y., & Yu, Y. (2004). An enhanced technology acceptance model for web-based learning. *Journal of Information Systems Education, 15*(4), 365–374.

Hassanzadeh, A., Kanaani, F., & Elahi, S. (2012). A model for measuring e-learning systems success in universities. *Expert Systems with Applications, 39*(12), 10959–10966.

Hayashi, A., Chen, C., Ryan, T., & Wu, J. (2004). The role of social presence and moderating role of computer self efficacy in predicting the continuance usage of e-learning systems. *Journal of Information Systems Education, 15,* 139–154.

Hayashi, A., Chen, C., Ryan, T., & Wu, J. (2004). The role of social presence and moderating role of computer self efficacy in predicting the continuance usage of e-learning systems. *Journal of Information Systems Education, 15*(2), 139.

Ho, C. L., & Dzeng, R. J. (2010). Construction safety training via e-learning: Learning effectiveness and user satisfaction. *Computers & Education, 55*(2), 858–867.

Holsapple, C. W., & Lee-Post, A. (2006). Defining, assessing, and promoting e-learning success: An information systems perspective. *Decision Sciences Journal of Innovative Education, 4*(1), 67–85.

Hong, S., Thong, J. Y., & Tam, K. Y. (2006). Understanding continued information technology usage behavior: A comparison of three models in the context of mobile Internet. *Decision Support Systems, 42*(3), 1819–1834.

Hsieh, P. A. J., & Cho, V. (2011). Comparing e-Learning tools' success: The case of instructor–student interactive vs. self-paced tools. *Computers & Education, 57*(3), 2025–2038.

Islam, A. N. (2011). The determinants of the post-adoption satisfaction of educators with an e-learning system. *Journal of Information Systems Education, 22*(4), 319.

Islam, A. N. (2013). Investigating e-learning system usage outcomes in the university context. *Computers & Education, 69,* 387–399.

Joo, Y. J., Lim, K. Y., & Kim, E. K. (2011). Online university students' satisfaction and persistence: Examining perceived level of presence, usefulness and ease of use as predictors in a structural model. *Computers & Education, 57*(2), 1654–1664.

Kang, Y. S., & Lee, H. (2010). Understanding the role of an IT artifact in online service continuance: An extended perspective of user satisfaction. *Computers in Human Behavior, 26*(3), 353–364.

Khan, B. (2005). Learning features in an open, flexible and distributed environment. *AACE Journal, 13*(2), 137–153.

Klobas, J. E., & McGill, T. J. (2010). The role of involvement in learning management system success. *Journal of Computing in Higher Education, 22*(2), 114–134.

Law, K. M., Lee, V. C., & Yu, Y. T. (2010). Learning motivation in e-learning facilitated computer programming courses. *Computers & Education, 55*(1), 218–228.

Leclercq, A. (2007). The perceptual evaluation of information systems using the construct of user satisfaction: Case study of a large French group. *ACM SIGMIS Database, 38*(2), 27–60.

Lee, B. C., Yoon, J. O., & Lee, I. (2009). Learners' acceptance of e-learning in South Korea: Theories and results. *Computers & Education, 53*(4), 1320–1329.

Lee, H., Choi, S. Y., & Kang, Y. S. (2009). Formation of e-satisfaction and repurchase intention: Moderating roles of computer self-efficacy and computer anxiety. *Expert Systems with Applications, 36*(4), 7848–7859.

Lee, J. K., & Lee, W. K. (2008). The relationship of e-learner's self-regulatory efficacy and perception of e-learning environmental quality. *Computers in Human Behavior, 24*(1), 32–47.

Lee, M. C. (2010). Explaining and predicting users' continuance intention toward e-learning: An extension of the expectation–confirmation model. *Computers & Education, 54*(2), 506–516.

Levy, Y. (2007). Comparing dropouts and persistence in e-learning courses. *Computers & Education, 48*(2), 185–204.

Liaw, S. S. (2001). Developing a user acceptance model for web-based learning. *Educational Technology, 41*(6), 50–54.

Liaw, S. S. (2008). Investigating students' perceived satisfaction, behavioural intention, and effectiveness of e-learning: A case study of the Blackboard system. *Computers & Education, 51*(2), 864–873.

Liaw, S. S., & Huang, H. M. (2013). Perceived satisfaction, perceived usefulness and interactive learning environments as predictors to self-regulation in e-learning environments. *Computers & Education, 60*(1), 14–24.

Liaw, S. S., Huang, H. M., & Chen, G. D. (2007). Surveying instructor and learner attitudes toward e-learning. *Computers & Education, 49*(4), 1066-1080.

Lim, H., Lee, S. G., & Nam, K. (2007). Validating e-learning factors affecting training effectiveness. *International Journal of Information Management, 27*(1), 22–35.

Limayem, M., & Cheung, C. M. K. (2008). Understanding information systems continuance: The case of Internet-based learning technologies. *Information & Management, 45*(4), 227–232.

Lin, H. F. (2008). Determinants of successful virtual communities: Contributions from system characteristics and social factors. *Information & Management, 45*(8), 522–527.

Lin, H. F. (2007). Measuring online learning systems success: Applying the updated DeLone and McLean model. *CyberPsychology & Behavior, 10*(6), 817–820.

Lin, H. F., & Lee, G. G. (2006). Determinants of success for online communities: an empirical study. *Behaviour & Information Technology, 25*(6), 479–488.

Liu, J. N., & Cheng, X. (2008). An evaluation of the learning of undergraduates using e-learning in a tertiary institution in China. *International Journal on ELearning, 7*(3), 427.

MacDonald, C. J., Stodel, E. J., Farres, L. G., Breithaupt, K., & Gabriel, M. A. (2001). The demand-driven learning model: A framework for web-based learning. *The Internet and Higher Education, 4*(1), 9–30.

Marangunić, N., & Granić, A. (2015). Technology acceptance model: A literature review from 1986 to 2013. *Universal Access in the Information Society, 14*(1), 81–95.

Martinez-Torres, M. R., Toral Marín, S. L., Garcia, F. B., Vazquez, S. G., Oliva, M. A., & Torres, T. (2008). A technological acceptance of e-learning tools used in practical and laboratory teaching, according to the European higher education area. *Behaviour & Information Technology, 27*(6), 495–505.

Martins, L. L., & Kellermanns, F. W. (2004). A model of business school students' acceptance of a web-based course management system. *Academy of Management Learning & Education, 3*(1), 7–26.

Masrek, M. N., Jamaludin, A., & Mukhtar, S. A. (2010). Evaluating academic library portal effectiveness: A Malaysian case study. *Library Review, 59*(3), 198–212.

McFarland, D. J. (2001, October). *The role of age and efficacy on technology acceptance: Implications for e-learning.* Paper presented at the World Conference on the WWW and Internet Proceedings, Orlando, FL.

Naveh, G., Tubin, D., & Pliskin, N. (2010). Student LMS use and satisfaction in academic institutions: The organizational perspective. *The Internet and Higher Education, 13*(3), 127–133.

Ngai, E. W. T., Poon, J. K. L., & Chan, Y. H. C. (2007). Empirical examination of the adoption of WebCT using TAM. *Computers & Education, 48*(2), 250–267.

Oliver, R. (2001). Assuring the quality of online learning in Australian higher education. In M. Walle, A. Ell, & D. Newton (Eds.), *Proceedings of Moving Online II conference* (pp. 222–31). Lismore, NSW, Australia.

Ong, C. S., & Lai, J. Y. (2006). Gender differences in perceptions and relationships among dominants of e-learning acceptance. *Computers in Human Behavior, 22*(5), 816–829.

Ong, C. S., & Lai, J. Y. (2007). Measuring user satisfaction with knowledge management systems: scale development, purification, and initial test. *Computers in Human Behavior, 23*(3), 1329–1346.

Ozkan, S., & Koseler, R. (2009). Multi-dimensional students' evaluation of e-learning systems in the higher education context: An empirical investigation. *Computers & Education, 53*(4), 1285–1296.

Oztekin, A., Kong, Z. J., & Uysal, O. (2010). UseLearn: A novel checklist and usability evaluation method for eLearning systems by criticality metric analysis. *International Journal of Industrial Ergonomics, 40*(4), 455–469.

Parker, M. A., & Martin, F. (2010). Using virtual classrooms: Student perceptions of features and characteristics in an online and blended course. *Journal of Online Learning and Teaching, 6*(1), 135.

Pawlowski, J. M., Barker, K. C., & Okamoto, T. (2007). Foreword: Quality research for learning, education, and training. *Educational Technology and Society, 10*(2), 1–2.

Phipps, R., & Merisotis, J. (2000). *Quality on the line: Benchmarks for success in Internet-based distance education* (Report No. 2000-175). Washington, DC: Institute for Higher Education Policy.

Piccoli, G., Ahmad, R., & Ives, B. (2001). Web-based virtual learning environments: A research framework and a preliminary assessment of effectiveness in basic IT skills training. *MIS Quarterly, 25*(4), 401–426.

Pike, R. H., Tayles, M. E., & Abu Mansor, N. N. (2010). Activity-based costing user satisfaction and type of system: A research note. *The British Accounting Review, 43*, 65–72.

Pituch, K. A., & Lee, Y. K. (2006). The influence of system characteristics on e-learning use. *Computers & Education, 47*(2), 222–244.

Ramayah, T., Ahmad, N. H., & Lo, M. C. (2010). The role of quality factors in intention to continue using an e-learning system in Malaysia. *Procedia Social and Behavioural Sciences, 2*(2), 5422–5426.

Roca, J. C., Chiu, C. M., & Martínez, F. J. (2006). Understanding e-learning continuance intention: An extension of the technology acceptance model. *International Journal of Human-Computer Studies, 64*(8), 683–696.

Rosenberg, M. J. (2006). Beyond e-learning. *Approaches and technologies to enhance organizational knowledge, learning, and performance*. San Francisco, CA: Pfeiffer.

Sánchez, R. A., & Hueros, A. D. (2010). Motivational factors that influence the acceptance of Moodle using TAM. *Computers in Human Behavior, 26*(6), 1632–1640.

Selim, H. M. (2003). An empirical investigation of student acceptance of course websites. *Computers & Education, 40*(4), 343–360.

Selim, H. M. (2007). Critical success factors for e-learning acceptance: Confirmatory factor models. *Computers & Education, 49*(2), 396–413.

Shee, D. Y., & Wang, Y. S. (2008). Multi-criteria evaluation of the web-based e-learning system: A methodology based on learner satisfaction and its applications. *Computers & Education, 50*(3), 894–905.

Sørum, H., Andersen, K. N., & Vatrapu, R. (2012). Public websites and human-computer interaction: An empirical study of measurement of website quality and user satisfaction. *Behaviour & Information Technology, 31*(7), 697–706.

Ssemugabi, S., & De Villiers, R. (2007). A comparative study of two usability evaluation methods using a web-based e-learning application. In *Proceedings of the 2007 annual research conference of the South African institute of computer scientists and information technologists on IT research in developing countries* (pp. 132–142). New York, NY: ACM.

Stoel, L., & Lee, K. H. (2003). Modeling the effect of experience on student acceptance of web-based courseware. *Internet Research, 13*(5), 364–374.

Sun, P. C., Tsai, R. J., Finger, G., Chen, Y. Y., & Yeh, D. (2008). What drives a successful e-learning? An empirical investigation of the critical factors influencing learner satisfaction. *Computers & Education, 50*(4), 1183–1202.

Taha, M. (2014). *Investigating the success of e-learning in secondary schools: The case of the Kingdom of Bahrain* (Doctoral dissertation). Brunel University, London, England.

Toral, S. L., Barrero, F., & Martínez-Torres, M. R. (2007). Analysis of utility and use of a web-based tool for digital signal processing teaching by means of a technological acceptance model. *Computers & Education, 49*(4), 957–975.

Volery, T., & Lord, D. (2000). Critical success factors in online education. *International Journal of Educational Management, 14*(5), 216–223.

Wang, H. C., & Chiu, Y. F. (2011). Assessing e-learning 2.0 system success. *Computers & Education, 57*(2), 1790–1800.

Wang, W. T., & Wang, C. C. (2009). An empirical study of instructor adoption of web-based learning systems. *Computers & Education, 53*(3), 761–774.

Wang, Y. S., & Liao, Y. W. (2008). Assessing eGovernment systems success: A validation of the DeLone and McLean model of information systems success. *Government Information Quarterly, 25*(4), 717–733.

Wang, Y. S., Wang, H. Y., & Shee, D. Y. (2007). Measuring e-learning systems success in an organisational context: Scale development and validation. *Computers in Human Behavior, 23*(4), 1792–1808.

Wu, J. H., Tennyson, R. D., Hsia, T. L., & Liao, Y. W. (2008). Analysis of e-learning innovation and core capability using a hypercube model. *Computers in Human Behavior, 24*(5), 1851–1866.

Yi, M. Y., & Hwang, Y. (2003). Predicting the use of web-based information systems: Self-efficacy, enjoyment, learning goal orientation, and the technology acceptance model. *International Journal of Human-Computer Studies, 59*(4), 431–449.

Zaharias, P., & Poulymenakou, A. (2003). Identifying training needs for ICT skills enhancement in south-eastern Europe: Implications for designing web-based training courses. *Educational Technology & Society, 6*(1), 50–54.

Zaíane, O. R. (2002). Building a recommender agent for e-learning systems. In *Proceedings of the International Conference on Computers in Education* (pp. 55–59). Auckland, New Zealand.

THE EESS MODEL HAS 52 MEASURES GROUPED UNDER 7 CONSTRUCTS FOR MEASURING THE SUCCESS OF E-LEARNING SYSTEMS.

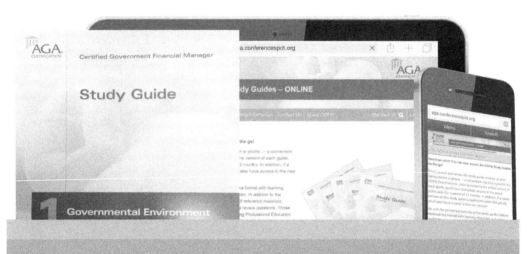

Ends and Means

Teaching Online Postsecondary Students With a Disability, Chronic Health Condition, or Mental or Emotional Illness
Resources for Instructors

Natalie B. Milman

Natalie B. Milman,
Associate Professor,
Graduate School of Education and Human
Development, The George Washington
University, 2134 G ST, NW, Washington, DC
20052. Telephone: (202) 994-1884.
E-mail: nmilman@gwu.edu

As an asynchronous online educator, it is important to cultivate a learning community where all learners feel welcome, supported, and able to thrive. For me, part of this involves incorporating differentiated instruction (Milman, 2009; Tomlinson, 2017) and universal design for learning (Meyer, Rose, & Gordon, 2014). Occasionally it also involves incorporating accommodations for students who have a disability, chronic health condition, or mental or emotional illness. In fact, the number of students with learning disabilities (Belkin, 2018) and/or mental health issues (Belkin, 2018; New, 2017) is expected to grow in institutions of higher education. Each of these conditions poses unique challenges for students and may also exacerbate others; therefore, it is important to understand not only the condition, but also how to design instruction and use adaptations that promote students' success, no matter their challenge(s).

Most institutions of higher education have developed processes for documenting and supporting students with disabilities through a disability support services office or center. In many institutions of higher education, students can register their disability to ensure they receive needed support. Because the process may vary from institution-to-institution, it is important for both students and instructors, particularly those who advise students, to become familiar with the procedures "to ensure that [their] accommodations are appropriately and efficiently communicated to university faculty and other necessary parties" ("Registration," n.d., para. 2). For example, at the George Washington University, students must register with the office of Disability Support Services (DSS, https://disability-support.gwu.edu/) **each term** and with **each instructor**. It is also the student's responsibility to "notify [their] professors that [they] are registered with Disability Support Services and that [they] are entitled to the accommodations for which DSS has deemed [them to be] eligible" ("Letters to Professors," n.d., para. 1).

Notifying instructors each term is a tedious task and for many students it is a daunting process to have to repeat each term and with each instructor (Alyssa, 2017). Some may feel ashamed or concerned they will be singled out or treated differently. Consequently, it is important for instructors to encourage students to register if they need accommodations and then to schedule meetings and/or conference calls to determine how best to meet their needs.

The student meeting or conference to discuss the accommodations is important because the needed accommodations vary from student to student (even those with the same challenges), as well as helps determine a plan for incorporating the necessary accommodations. During such discussions, students should describe which accommodations are needed and together, the student and instructor should develop and document the accommodation plan (this could be as simple as a follow-up email or a more formal learning contract). It is also recommended to check in with the student throughout the term or semester to see how things are going and to determine if any other accommodations or changes are needed. This way, instructors and students maintain an ongoing dialog.

Instructors should also seek help from their office of disability support services and/or other resources, especially considering that most faculty have not had much, if any, preparation learning how to teach, let alone how to support students needing accommodations. Below are some resources to learn more.

ONLINE RESOURCES

- **AEM for Higher Education Faculty** (http://aem.cast.org/about/quick-start-higher-education-postsecondary-faculty.html#.W7-mmxNKit8)—Developed by the National Center for Accessible Materials, this site houses accessible educational materials for higher education faculty to use.
- **Association for Higher Education and Disability** (https://www.ahead.org/home)—This is an association focused on individuals (e.g., faculty, student affairs personnel), who support higher education students with disabilities.
- **Federal agencies and federally funded centers working on disability and higher education** (https://www.nccsdclearinghouse.org/federal-agencies.html)—This is a directory of federal agencies and federally-funded centers working on disability and higher education.
- **National Alliance on Mental Health** (https://www.nami.org/Find-Support)—

This site has numerous resources related to mental health support.

- **National Center for College Students with Disabilities Clearinghouse** (https://www.nccsdclearinghouse.org/)—Search for resources such as peer-reviewed articles about disability and higher education.
- **National Organizations Working on Disability and Higher Education** (https://www.nccsdclearinghouse.org/national-organizations.html)—This is a clearinghouse of organizations working on disability and higher education.

PRINT RESOURCES

Harbour, W. S., & Greenberg, D. (2017, July). Campus climate and students with disabilities. *NCCSD Research Brief, 1*(2). Huntersville, NC: National Center for College Students with Disabilities, Association on Higher Education and Disability. Retrieved from http://www.nccsdonline.org/uploads/7/6/7/7/7677280/nccsd_campus_climate_brief_-_final_pdf_with_tags2.pdf

McAlvage, K., & Rice, M. (2018). *Access and accessibility in online learning issues in higher education and k–12 contexts.* OLC Research Center for Digital Learning & Leadership. Retrieved from https://onlinelearningconsortium.org/read/access-and-accessibility-in-online-learning

REFERENCES

Alyssa. (2017, November 26) *Disabled in grad school: I, too, dread the accommodations talk: A student's perspective on discussing accommodations.* Retrieved from https://www.insidehighered.com/blogs/gradhacker/disabled-grad-school-i-too-dread-accommodations-talk

Belkin, D. (2018, May 24). Colleges bend the rules for more students, give them extra help. In *Wall Street Journal.* Retrieved from https://www.wsj.com/articles/colleges-bend-the-rules-for-more-students-give-them-extra-help-1527154200

Letters to Professors. (n.d.). In *Disability Support Services.* Retrieved from https://disabilitysupport.gwu.edu/letters-professors

Meyer, A., Rose, D. H., & Gordon, D. (2014). *Universal design for learning: Theory and practice.* Wakefield, MA: CAST.

Milman, N. B. (2009). Differentiating instruction in online environments. *Distance Learning, 6*(3), 87–89.

New, J. (2017, January 13). Balancing response and treatment. In *Inside Higher Education.* Retrieved from https://www.insidehighered.com/news/2017/01/13/colleges-struggle-provide-ongoing-treatment-demands-mental-health-services-increases

Registration. (n.d.). In *Disability Support Services.* Retrieved from https://disabilitysupport.gwu.edu/registration

Tomlinson, C. A. (2017). *How to differentiate instruction in academically diverse classrooms* (3rd ed.). Alexandria, VA: ASCD.

IT IS IMPORTANT TO CULTIVATE A LEARNING COMMUNITY WHERE ALL LEARNERS FEEL WELCOME, SUPPORTED, AND ABLE TO THRIVE.

Try This

The Great Pitchman
Selling Distance Learning to the Hesitant Student

Errol Craig Sull

This is a column that is long overdue, and one I've had many calls to write: giving solid reasons why a student taking an online course for the first time should welcome it, not fear it. As much as online education has become commonplace there are still many students who have not experienced an online course, and this step into unchartered waters can appear somewhat daunting at first. Of course, we who teach online know the many plusses of an online class. Take the points I've outlined here and share them with your students: no doubt at least a few will probably be new to online education, and one or items I've listed make hit home with them.

How to have a great time with online education:

EMBRACE THE COURSE

You'll be taking an online course, so don't fight, don't complain—love it! This may sound weird, but if you approach the course with a mindset of "This is really going to be cool!" you'll find a better focus on the course innards and less concern about "Oh, man—an online course: what do I do now?! Bottom line: dive in, with the idea this is going to be one of the best learning experiences you've had—because it can be!

THE MORE FAMILIAR, THE MORE RELAXED

New city, new job, new school—all can make you a bit unnerved, all can make someone feel a tad frazzled. Taking your

Errol Craig Sull,
Full-Time Faculty, English,
American InterContinental University.
E-mail: ESull@aiuniv.edu
and erroldistancelearning@gmail.com
(for column submissions)

first online course can be the same: suddenly, there is no door, there are no seats, there is no physical professor. Yet just as with anything new, the more we get to know it the more comfortable we feel. So ... explore every nook and cranny of your online course—read thoroughly the syllabus—get to know due dates—find course and school resources and (if applicable) the eBook text—learn how to contact the professor, how to submit assignments, how to handle discussion postings. All this will quickly make your first online course seem like a neighborhood where you've lived a long time!

GREAT SUPPORT—AND 24/7

"How do I do this?" ... "This assignment is a bit confusing to me" ... "Oh, oh—this live link in my course does not open!" ..."Can you explain this feedback comment on my assignment more thoroughly?": these and many other questions and "unexpecteds" may come up in your online course—but help is available for what seems 24/7! You can call or e-mail (and sometimes text and instant message) your instructor at any time, with a prompt response—technical support is usually available any time of the day—and helpful videos, fact sheets, and/ or frequently asked questions (with answers) postings abound throughout the course. And you always have a great safety net: your advisor. This friendly and helpful person will be with you throughout your years in school, and is a constant resource for questions, concerns, and problems.

REVISIT, REVISIT, REVISIT

Ah, how nice to have available every word mentioned by a professor, each discussion posting of classmates, all feedback on assignments, every school library book— and all readily accessible in one easy-to-navigate location! Your online course gives you this, as everything that is associated with your course is always available in print, video, and/or audio. And since this all exists on your computer screen there is no wandering, to travel, no wait time, no "Do you remember what was said?" Every component of the course—no matter how big or small—is quickly available to you.

IMPROVE YOUR WRITING ABILITY— NO MATTER THE COURSE

There are two life skills where you are judged by others nearly every day: public speaking and writing. And writing—good writing—is a skill you need for every course you take, as well as on an almost daily basis in the professional world. In an online course you are always writing: major assignments and discussion postings, e-mails, and possible group summaries, interactive personalized learning system questions, quizzes, et cetera. These equate to a whole bunch of writing, and while your professor will give you feedback on some to help you improve (and more, depending on the course, such as English), other course-related writing you do will be practice, with sometimes feedback from classmates. All of this will help you become a better writer—and a writer judged nicely by others!

LEARN HOW TO EAT ANXIETY AND STRESS FOR BREAKFAST

An online course doesn't differ much from other courses in the anxiety and stress getting in assignments and working toward a good grade produce. There are so many nice options, however, that can minimize any of these negatives you might feel. First, as much as possible, have an environment around you where it's more conducive to doing your online course—this brings about an "Ah!" factor. Next, always look for outlets to relax the mind and/or body. These could be as simple as stretching, watching a TV show, or eating a piece of chocolate to taking a walk, going to the gym for a workout, or playing with a baby/ having an activity with a family member. Any of these will put you back in your online class more relaxed. And stress and anxiety? Well, they will have melted away!

DISCUSSION: A BIG PLUS FOR "THE REAL WORLD"

Discussion in an online course is often referred to as the "heartbeat" of the class, and for good reason: it is live interchange between students and students, between students and professor. And when you post to discussion your responses should never be "That's good," "I agree," "Nice idea," et cetera, as comments like this tell the person reading your post ... nothing! Rather, you want to give the same type of feedback you'd like to receive from others: detailed, so it can prove helpful. This is the feedback you are expected to give colleagues in the professional world—discussion feedback that can really help with a problem, a product, a customer—anything relating to the business. Discussion in an online class is perfect training ground for this, so remember: make your posts intelligent and well-thought-out posts—these are what your classmates and professor will respect, these are what your work colleagues and employer will appreciate.

YOU CAN FORGET ABOUT THE EVILS OF NATURE

"I don't want to leave for school today: the snow is coming down quite heavily" ... "Oh, no, it's really, really raining—and I don't have an umbrella to help me off to school" ... "There is a mudslide that cut off access to my school—how do I get there" ..."It's 5 below zero with a fierce wind—no way do I want to venture out to school today": these and other weather-related comments are fairly common when one is attending a school with a physical presence of classrooms. But when taking an online course all of these evils of nature sit quietly on a shelf, as you have your entire course—your entire school—on a computer screen just a few inches in front of you. Sure, networks go down every now

and then, but they quickly pop up—and you've lost very little time in the classroom. You can smile!

TAKE IT WHEREVER YOU GO

Our society is more mobile than ever, traveling from city to city, country to country; moving from one job to another; having hobbies and outside interests causing us to go hither and yon; and we leaving one neighborhood in our city and taking up residence in another neighborhood. "Back in the day," before online courses, you couldn't do much with your class unless you were at your school or home ... but as Zorba the Greek once remarked, "That was then, this is now"! With an online course you can take it just about anywhere: to the tops of mountains, inside parks, during a lunch break, on a fishing jaunt, to a baseball game, from a previous house to a new one, on the job—the list is almost endless. And added to laptops and tablets are school apps that make your course as available as your cell phone is with you. All of this results in an online course that is convenient to take— and gives you more time to do it.

TIME EXPANDS— BUT DO MANAGE IT

An online course allows access on an anytime, anywhere basis—but this seemingly endless supply of time always has finite endings: due dates of assignments and discussion postings, as well as "must do by" date for other class activities. A great way to stay on top of this is by creating a timeline for yourself—it will tell you when to do the class readings, to start and submit assignments, to post discussions, etc. It's your little guide to keep you on track with each component of your online class—you never want time to get the best of you, but rather you want to be the one controlling it.

Remember: Something is new until you touch it, then it becomes old, familiar, and like a good friend.

Volume 19, Number 2, 2018

Quarterly Review
OF Distance
Education

RESEARCH THAT GUIDES PRACTICE

Editors:
Michael Simonson
Charles Schlosser

≡IAP
INFORMATION AGE
PUBLISHING

An Official Journal of the
Association for Educational Communications and Technology

QUARTERLY REVIEW OF DISTANCE EDUCATION,
SUBSCRIBE TODAY!
WWW.INFOAGEPUB.COM

Ask Errol!

Errol Craig Sull

Distance learning always morphs, is always changing, and with these come new teaching strategies, student challenges, course maneuvering, and a gaggle of "unexpecteds"! The questions on how to handle these keep coming to me, and I'll always try my best to give the best advice possible. Three more are in this column, and I look forward to hearing from you! (Please send me your questions to erroldistancelearning@gmail.com.)

Here are the issues—and my suggestions.

Errol Craig Sull,
Full-Time Faculty, English,
American InterContinental University.
E-mail: ESull@aiuniv.edu
and erroldistancelearning@gmail.com
(for column submissions)

My classes are going well, Errol, and part of that I owe to you for the valuable info you've given me over the years, But I've encountered a problem I've never had: a student who is so eager to be seen in discussion he not only continually posts (as an example: our school requires students post four times per week, and one week he posted 18 times!) but has taken on the role of a somewhat teacher's aide, reminding other students what to do, and correcting their writing and any facts they get wrong (I teach a freshman history class). He has never been mean, but some students are complaining to me they are hesitant to post because of this student. Any suggestions?

Thanks so much for the positive feedback—it's always nice to know my advice is helping other online educators! As to your "problem" student, I've had a few of those in my years of teaching distance learning, and the reason they do this varies: some want to merely be seen as a "teacher's pet," others need the attention of being seen all the time, and still a few simply believe their actions are good ones. What I have done in all cases is, first, send the student an e-mail (of course, you would never mention anything in your discussion posting—it would be embarrassing to the student), and explain how balance in a classroom is very important, that when someone dominates the discussion it often can make others feel there is no room for them, and an equal exchange of ideas is important. Also, mention that while you appreciate his help in students' writing and history facts it comes across to others as being a bully—something with which he would never want to be associated. Also: ask him how he would feel if the roles were revered, not only in the classroom but also in the professional world. And certainly, if the e-mail does not work call him—in nearly all cases when I had little luck with e-mails the phone calls did the trick!

Errol, I reach out to my students on a constant basis, through emails, texting, and phone calls, and this has helped me create a good bond with many of my students. Although corresponding on many issues— nearly all related to the class—over the years I've had some students reveal some rather disturbing reasons as to why they have not been more active in class or why they previously failed the course. Domestic abuse, being homeless, divorce, severe family illness or death in the family, the students' major disability, and house burned down are some of these. I try my best to respond, but sometimes I think there is more that I could do. Any help you can give me would be greatly appreciated.

It wasn't until I started teaching online, and thus had more e-mail and pretty much first-time phone contact with students, that I started hearing similar info from my students. A few items: (1) Check to see if your school has any policy on whom to contact in the event of a problem that sounds life-threatening. (I once had a student who told me she was so depressed she was contemplating suicide. I immediately contacted the student's advisor, who contacted the police in her area; they checked on her, and determined she did need help, which she received.) (2) Tell the student how you will help him or her overcome the challenge to being more involved in the classroom—and when I say "tell" I mean through one of the means you mention: a phone call. That personal exchange

is crucial in getting to student to, in essence, lean on your shoulder with classroom work. This often takes more than one call, but in my experience this helps the majority of these students. (3) Never—and I mean NEVER—get into any discussion about the personal problems the students have; that is not your role. Only focus on how you are going to work with the students to overcome the problems for better class involvement. (4) Cover yourself: let your supervisor and the student's advisor know of the problem any student relayed to you. Doing all of these suggestions will allow you to have the best efforts with these students while knowing you've done everything on your end to help them and yourself.

I like to think I give good feedback on assignments, Errol, and over the years you've mentioned a few items that touched on this, which I've incorporated into my feedback. But are there any surefire tricks or tips you can give so my feedback on students' assignments stands out as excellent? I teach two different psychology courses, and many of my students are psychology majors. Some will certainly go into that field, but the majority probably not.

I'm pleased to know that some of my info has squirreled its way into your feedback efforts—thanks! Feedback is critical, of course, as students depend on it to improve their next assignments and, hopefully, it will help them in "the real world." For my feedback I always use a five-part approach: (1) Indicate to the student something he or she wrote is incorrect. And I always try to use words that are by no means demeaning but can best be described as "constructive criticism." (2) Next, I let the student know why what was written is incorrect, and I explain it not as a professor talking down to a student but rather as a person just trying to explain a problem to another. (3) I then let the student know how to "get it right"—this is mandatory, because no feedback is worth anything without help to improve. (4) I always have an overall comment to the student (crucial, as it shows you are not a robot, but rather a teacher who cares!) and included in this is how what the student wrote—topic and/or the student's writing ability—relates to the professional world in which the student will be spending most of his or her days. (5) In my individual items feedback I often include helpful websites on more information relating to the item, and I have a general list of help-ful websites at the bottom of the assign-ments. This approach has resulted in kudos from my supervisors and students for many years—and I know the same will happen for you!

Remember: Haircuts look better when given by a barber, lawnmowers cut better when a professional sharpens their blades, and paintings take on a *je ne sais qua* when taught by an art instructor. Others helping us improve is a nice little bonus of life.

PROVIDING HELPFUL WEBSITES AT THE BOTTOM OF ASSIGNMENTS IS APPRECIATED BY STUDENTS.

Get Your Copy Today—Information Age Publishing

And Finally ... *continued from page 88*

Niss (2016) attempted to clarify what is meant by the digital curriculum by stating that the six factors that make up the curriculum are: goals, content, materials, forms of teaching, student activities, and assessment. These six must become digital in order to offer a truly digital curriculum.

The process by which education moves from the traditional artifacts of curriculum to a digital curriculum is a hierarchical process. At the base of the hierarchy is the written curriculum of the traditional educational system. At the apex is the student and teacher surrounded by a virtual, digital curriculum world where all materials are available, any form of teaching is possible, alternative and unimagined student activities are expected, and assessment is determined by artifacts. Artifacts are student created outcomes of digital learning.

And finally, as T.S. Eliot wrote, the best in listening to music, is when music is "heard so *deeply* that it is not heard at all, but *you* are the music, while the music lasts." The advocates of the deeply digital curriculum say that; it is not noticed at all, the students are the curriculum, while the curriculum lasts?

REFERENCES

Niss, M. (2016). *Digital curricula in school mathematics.* Charlotte, NC: Information Age.

President's Council of Advisors on Science and Technology. (2010). *Prepare and inspire: K–12 education in science, technology, engineering, and math (STEM) for America's future: Executive report.* Executive Office of the President, President's Council of Advisors on Science and Technology. Washington, DC: Author.

IN A DEEPLY DIGITAL COURSE, THE TEACHER AND STUDENT ARE SURROUNDED BY A VIRTUAL, DIGITAL CURRICULUM WORLD WHERE ALL MATERIALS ARE AVAILABLE, ANY FORM OF TEACHING IS POSSIBLE, ALTERNATIVE AND UNIMAGINED STUDENT ACTIVITIES ARE EXPECTED, AND ASSESSMENT IS DETERMINED BY STUDENT PRODUCED ARTIFACTS.

And Finally ...

Let's Go Deeply Digital?

Michael Simonson

The origination of the term "deeply digital" is widely credited to a Report to the President made in 2010 by the President's Council of Advisors on Science and Technology. The core of this report was that technology, deeply digital technology,

> should not replace teachers but support them. Properly used, technology can extend the reach of teachers by giving them access to the best instructional and professional development tools that can create customized learning environ-

Michael Simonson, Editor, *Distance Learning,* and Program Professor, Programs in Instructional Technology and Distance Education, Fischler School of Education, Nova Southeastern University, 3301 College Avenue, Fort Lauderdale, FL 33314. Telephone: (954) 262-8563. E-mail: simsmich@nsu.nova.edu

ments and assessments for students, and to capture rich information about individual performance. (p. 80)

The report emphasized the power of communities, open courseware, electronic textbooks, tutoring systems, and online courses. Goals for education, it said, should promote:

- development of common technology platforms;
- development of deeply digital whole course materials;
- development of modular instructional materials;
- development of innovative assessments
- rapid prototyping;
- data mining;
- broad dissemination;
- innovative procurement; and
- consortia.

Many now consider that to go deeply digital is to be immersive, innovative, and nontraditional in the use of digital instructional technologies in teaching and learning. A new companion phrase—digital curriculum—has also emerged in the literature. The two terms—deeply digital and digital curriculum—are related because, when an educational organization goes deeply digital, it is within the framework of the digital curriculum.

... continues on page 87

CPSIA information can be obtained
at www.ICGtesting.com
Printed in the USA
FFHW011422030219
50391432-55534FF